LIVING IN THE BACKWATERS

By
Michael Emmett

GAFF RIG PUBLICATIONS
MALDON, ESSEX

First published by GAFF RIG PUBLICATIONS 1996

GAFF RIG PUBLICATIONS
OSTREA ROSE THE HYTHE MALDON ESSEX CM9 7HN

ISBN 0 9529554 0 7

Printed by The Bath Press, Bath
Reprographics by Mikro, Tiptree, Essex
Production Co-ordinator and Marketing – G. A. Pitt, Layer De La Haye

DEDICATED TO DEBORAH
a true Blackwater woman

I would like to thank Jan Whitley for her hours of hard labour preparing the manuscript, along with my friends and charter guests who kindly provided many of the photographs.

Thanks also must go to everyone involved in making this style of life possible, independent and individualistic characters, who shine in this modern world of standardisation and stereotype.

Sail with us and absorb the experience:
Ostrea Rose The Hythe Maldon CM9 7HN
Telephone: 01621 841321/01245 261362

INTRODUCTION

The Essex coast has long been a breeding ground for good sailors. That is sailors in the true sense of the word; men who went to sea in ships propelled by the wind. The hey day of Essex sail was the 1890s until around 1910 when each river had its own particular types of sailing craft. Around Southend it was small sailing barges carrying freights into the lonely creeks while in the summer tripper boats took holiday makers for a short bash across the Thames mouth. At Leigh there was the famous fleet of bawleys sailing each summer morning into the estuary in the pursuit of shrimps.

The Crouch and the Roach were, apart from oysters, smacks and a few sailing barges a wild tranquil area, while Maldon at the head of the Blackwater was a busy little port with coal arriving from the north of England and timber from the Baltic. Down at West Mersea oysters kept a little fleet of small smacks busy in the local creeks. Tollesbury also had a fleet of sailing smacks roaming around the Thames Estuary, while Brightlingsea at the mouth of the River Colne was a thriving fishing centre. Smacks from here sailed around the British coast and the 'skillingers' crossed the North Sea to dredge oysters off the island of Terschelling. A hard and dangerous way to earn a living.

There were smacks further up the Colne at Wivenhoe and Rowhedge, but this was really the home of professional yachting. According to local legend the yachting dates back to the famous racing cutter Pearl built at Wivenhoe in 1820. It seems that the Marquis of Anglesey heard that very fast smuggling craft were built by one Phillip Sainty. The Marquis found that Sainty was in jail for smuggling and he had to pay his fine to get him out. Sainty promptly said he could not build the noble Marquis a fast yacht unless he had his brother-in-law bought out of jail as well. The Marquis did the decent thing and paid the brother-in-laws fine as well. This incident seems to have established two local traditions, building fast boats and taking money off the gentry. Up until the 1920s the main economy of Wivenhoe and Rowhedge was building and manning yachts for the aristocracy and the new competitive breed of rich industrialists.

To complete the survey of the golden age, the port of Colchester was mostly sailing barge trade, while the lonely Walton Backwaters was a smaller version of the Blackwater. In the late nineteenth century a number of large mills and maltings were built on Mistley quay, all supplied by water, and this lead to Fred Horlock creating the only large coastal shipping fleet in Essex. Horlock not only built and operated sailing barges, but went on to operate steam ships in the ocean trades. There were steam ships and steam yachts in Essex, but mostly there were small individually owned sailing craft.

The Essex coast is protected from really bad onshore gales by the off lying sand banks and this created an area where ageing wooden sailing craft could go on working long after they were abandoned in other parts of Britain. In the 1950s and into the 1960s there were numerous old sailing craft about in the Thames Estuary. There were even more elderly men who had sailed on them and were only too willing to talk about the golden age of coastal sail. Anyone who was about then could not help feeling sorry that these wonderful craft were about to vanish for ever.

The starting of the Maldon Barge race in 1962 triggered off the traditional sail revival movement. Suddenly people realised that the old barges and smacks did not have to be run up on the saltings and abandoned, instead they could be rebuilt and go on sailing. It was like starting a forest fire, everyone was looking for old boats to restore. Michael Emmett, a romantic who likes to sail his own course in life was bound to be caught up in the traditional sail scene.

Michael's first book, *Blackwater Men,* tells the story of how his family worked smacks from Maldon and his own career as a fisherman. It was as a professional fisherman that he had the smack *Ostrea Rose* built at Heybridge for oyster dredging in Lawlings Creek. This smack's design, like its owner, is firmly rooted in the past. However in the early 1980s an oyster disease swept through the Blackwater making it impossible for commercial oyster fishing to continue.

Michael then turned to charter work, hiring out the *Ostrea Rose* to people wishing to have a holiday afloat. This book covers the years of chartering and taking part in traditional boat races and rallies. The story told here is not of a holiday business, *Ostrea Rose* is run as a way of life. It is a life many might envy, sailing in the summer, but the long cold winter's aboard the smack with little income needs a tough outlook. None of this gets the master of *Ostrea Rose* down. A dry sense of humour and the fisherman's belief that tomorrow their luck will turn is the philosophy behind this most readable personal story.

Robert Simper

CONTENTS

MN 183

NEW BEGINNINGS

The direction for me over the ten years covered by this book is due initially to a man named Barry, a chance remark, and what I thought of at the time as a joke.

To explain, I think we must start in the Jolly Sailor public house at the Hythe, Maldon in 1982. Barry, whom I was drinking with, had moved into a house about four doors away from where I lived in Church Street. From this address I retailed fish to supplement the wholesale shellfish business I was running. Our first encounter was a transaction containing some smoked haddock, a great deal of chat and an agreement to rendezvous in the bar later. He was an ideas man, he never stopped. It was this quality about his company that was to carve the events to come. His sense of humour was an element that made an otherwise dull affair into an occasion, by drawing other

As the tripper never views Maldon.

(note: pulling skiff, Mayland Oyster and Ostrea Rose on the Bath Wall.)

(Opposite page) The early years. Picture by Keith Yuill

(a) Ostrea Rose as a loaded motor smack (with her sailing gear laid ashore).

(b) Sieving and culling.

(c) Winkles being washed.

peoples, lighter sides into the arena. As I am not one for being formal I just accepted that his name was Barry and that, as he told me, his dad made wagonwheels. It must have been nearly two years later that someone remarked about his surname being Burton.

So here I was sitting in a four ale bar with a hippie possessing a psychology degree, an inane sense of humour, and by this time a fish round for which I supplied the stock. The discussion in waterfront bars invariably ends up about boats and this discussion was not going to be any different. The `writing was on the wall', as they say, for making a living from commercial fishing on the Blackwater even at this early stage, the actual end coming some two years later. At this time I owned the smack *Ostrea Rose*, the bumkin, *Mayland Oyster* and two heavy clinker-built pulling skiffs. All of these were becoming redundant but unlike factories or machinery could not be pulled down or destroyed as boats become part of the family and you would hardly send your granny to the breakers. So during the conversation I posed the question: "What am I going to do with the vessels?" In his inimitable style Barry answered almost immediately, "Smuggling holidays". If that option has not yet been exploited commercially it certainly gave us a wealth of evening entertainment and laughter building castles in the sky, or were they?

The last commercial trip I made was to be with Barry as mate, although neither of us would have said before we went that that was to be the last, it just never happened again. We had been winkling and had brought up at Osea Island in the Barnacle to clean and bag the consignment when we saw some mullet along the edge of the mud. We made two shots, catching about a cwt. Towards the end of pulling in the net for the second time Barry said: "Smile you're in the movies". On looking up I saw a figure holding a video camera. Once we had cleaned the net and bagged the fish we rowed over to ask if it would be possible to see the footage at some point.

The gentleman, Mr Christmas, along with his wife entertained us extremely well with coffee and biscuits not forgetting the medicinal rum. We left some winkles, flounders and our contact address, waved goodbye and motored to Maldon to meet the lorry. A very long while later I received a copy of the video, on it was the footage of us followed by film which they had taken whilst on holiday up the Nile. There were Arabs catching the

(a) Mrs Nix's uncle built the shop onto the end of his house, when she found herself widowed with children at an early age in the late 1830's.

(b) The finishing touches.

same species of fish with a net looking almost identical to ours. I wonder if they still fish?

So the end came, not planned or calculated for but as swift as the headsman's axe. Although the dark clouds of the old hands prediction of 'Round O' had been building for many years, the optimism of the waterman, which is never dampened, believed that the inevitable would never really happen. When it did, it created a black void which at my age of just 34 had to be filled. For reasons beyond understanding now, I took on a project far detracted from the saltwater, I rebuilt a seventeenth-century house, which had an early Victorian Dutch façade, whilst my smack lay unattended in the saltings of Bradwell Creek. *Mayland Oyster* was sold and the last time I saw her was when I delivered her to a mooring in Buzzen at West Mersea. My gear was sold piecemeal and gradually disappeared, the rest falling apart from old age and heavy use, leaving very little of consequence from the shed-full once owned.

Barry reminded me of that cameo part in all good British film comedies: "I go, I come back". The one who always wore a fez and appeared to have nothing to do with the script but you always expected to see him. True to form he, Barry that is, disappeared from Maldon to reappear again later, and then again and again!

My stalwart workmate on this house project was a friend who had worked with me on the water, Paul Farrow. On and off for many years him and his shadow, a black cross-labrador, Peter, had been mate and third hand for me, whilst at times I went mate with him in his vessel, the *Moonlighter*. The first trip Peter made, he came aboard in Paul's jacket pocket but he soon grew and became larger than your average labrador. On one occasion in the wintertime we had decided to leave him ashore at Paul's home, a caravan nestled behind the sea wall at Steeple Creek. He had different ideas about this and was scanning the wall for us as we rowed away towards the smack out in Lawling Creek. I think he must have had lessons from Houdini because the chain on which we left him had a hard spring clip. Once he spotted us he leapt into the water which could have been little above freezing and started towards us. "Pull hard", said Paul, "he'll go back." We boarded, started the motor and let go the mooring. He was still coming. "Open her up, he'll definitely go back then." By this time we were almost to the main body of the river and there was no sign of him giving up. We, by this time, were very conscious that he had swum an awfully long way. It was us that gave in and picked him up. The look of achievement on that dog's face was overwhelming. I don't think we ever tried to leave him after that.

The three of us took up residence in the old building which had been treated, it seemed, with total neglect since its facia had been added about 1840. We sawed wood, laid bricks, dug holes, retiled roof elevations and plastered rooms. I think pointing brickwork must be the worst though, it even beats caulking a carvel-built boat. All this daily involvement still returned to talk of boats, fishing and gunning whilst we had our tea break, dinner, or night after night in The Green Man pub.

Paul Farrow boarding Ostrea Rose from the Moonlighter, both liberally covered in snow.

Then one day a letter came flooding in, it was from Barry. He had been using his education in a practise in Andover and had absorbed as much as he could take of other people's troubles and was asking for sanctuary. He wanted to 'play with a spade in the sand' and so joined us as a labourer. During this time he was moving his abode to Swansea and migrated back and forth about fortnightly. This was all very well except that we had going away parties and return parties fortnightly. His sense of humour had even beaten that house.

The building work was finished and fate took me further away from the salt water to lodge in Chelmsford with a lady who was extremely kind named Sue Backhouse. They say desperate situations breed definite action and at Sue's instigation I started the manuscript of my half of the book Blackwater Men. This at least allowed me the salt water in theory if not in practice. That winter, being totally without work, I applied for just about every position advertised to do with traditional vessels. I actually got offered three positions but turned them down. In fact I was so close to accepting one of them that I tossed a coin, heads I take it, tails I get Gayle Heard to make me a mainsail. The coin had hardly hit the floor when I made the telephone call to Gayle. The tide of inevitability had started to flood.

At sometime during that winter I placed an advertisement in one of the yachting magazines - "10 ton gaff-cutter requires crew, no pay, lots of sailing". I had a string of telephone calls from differing people all of which proved non fruitful, then the trail went cold. I returned temporarily to the tools and built Sue a large conservatory on her house. It was whilst hanging some patio doors that yet another letter came flooding in, yes, you guessed, it was from Barry. He was coming up to visit and had I thought any more about the smuggling holidays. It was also about this time that a telephone call came from a chap with a Hull accent, who said he had been given some back copies of magazines by his yacht club as they were throwing them away. He had noticed my advert and wondered what the plans were and if I was still looking for crew. I told him that there were no plans save sailing somewhere during the summer. We exchanged details and I said I would contact him should anything happen.

Barry arrived and in time honoured fashion we had a return party at The Cap and Feathers in Tillingham. We thought we would try the local brew, it was called S.A.S. On asking one of the regulars why it was so called he remarked: "If you have enough o' that you'll feel like you've bin trud on be a garrison o' sodgers." The next day, nursing a monumental hangover we went to get *Ostrea Rose* out of her mothballs.

She was a pretty bad sight, two and a half years of neglect. I think if I had been judge and jury I would have sentenced me to hard labour for allowing her to get in such a state. As it transpires, that which you sow, so shall you reap and she made us toil unmercifully. Finally, after about six weeks she started to look better than she ever did, especially adorned with her new mainsail. The day dawned when we could finally go somewhere, and we had to choose where. Although I had been a member of the Old Gaffers Association (OGA) back in the late sixties I had let my membership lapse long since, so I rejoined. The package received gave information about regattas, festivals and general boat gatherings. The first on the agenda was the Crouch Rally but the one that looked the most attractive was the first Classic Boat Festival at Shotley Marina which was to last over a week. It was decided that we should sail to Maldon, victual the ship and then set forth for Burnham.

We moored at the town quay alongside the new floating pontoon, well it does when the tide is up! I went 'up the town' as shopping is always referred to by Maldoners whilst Barry practised an art which he promised he would teach me, relaxation. When I returned I saw a notice hanging in the rigging which read: "Traditional Charter, Day Trips and Cruises, apply aboard." This triggered my sense of humour and reminded me of all those evenings discussing smuggling holidays, as if we had been playing Monopoly, and I started to laugh. Barry opened one eye and said: "Oh ye of little faith, I have taken a

The chalk board at Maldon Quay being tended by Melvin Parish. The smack alongside is Lizzie Annie, by this time owned by Bob Fawkes.

booking for two at the weekend". The joke had become a reality, maybe not quite like our preconceptions but it was a start.

The weekend was planned in the head of one of our guests to include a meal at a particular restaurant in Wivenhoe. As with so many plans of mice and men, OR saltwater, they do not always come to fruition. Sometimes, because things are too much in your favour rather than trying to stop you. The idea, as I see it, with cruising is to have a nice sail, under pleasant conditions, with good company, arriving at an interesting landfall just in time to enjoy an evening ashore. Of course, there are always those times when the wind shifts on to your head, the ensuing tacking making you late, which then fetches a foul tide down upon you and your landfall becomes 0400hrs or something. For all that, those times funnily enough are still enjoyed.

Anyway, this Saturday saw a northerly force 3-4 which fetched us to the mouth of the Colne before the day had hardly got going. A quick debate as to the circumstance at hand resulted in a unanimous decision to square away south, and take the Ray Sand Channel over into the Crouch before we lost too much depth to the ebb. Just inside Shore End, which is the start of the sea wall on the north side we saw a shape which through binoculars we identified as a pram dinghy. As the area is miles from anywhere and we could see neither yacht nor human life to which it could belong, we decided to investigate. Echoes of smuggling holidays started. Having brought the smack hove-to, underbowing the tide to maintain her station, our charterers were taken with this almost piratical type manoeuvre. This along with the pulling boat being sculled to the shore equipped with kedge anchors and long warps to facilitate an offing, it led, with a little assistance from Barry, to us feeling like we were after Captain Flint's treasure rather than a stray dinghy. Still that's showbiz, I enjoyed it and by the conversation in the Star pub later so did our guests. The idea worked.

As for the dinghy, we reported it to the Police and took it back to Maldon. A couple of days later we learnt that it belonged to a policeman from West Mersea, where it had got loose from the hard and had taken itself right across the Back of the Main before depositing itself upon the wall. He collected it in due course and our salvage rights amounted to two jars of his own honey and a £5 note. Circumstance and fate can sometimes save you from your own desires and it certainly proved helpful that weekend. Had we foregone the long sail for a day on the Wivenhoe mud we would have found that our guests restaurant was unavailable due to it having been shut down some weeks earlier.

Flush with success we planned our next trip. It was to be the Crouch Rally on the May bank-holiday. Again we found guests to accompany us, which included the young man from Hull, whom fate, I can only assume, had made him telephone just in time to join us. He arrived head first down the companion way announcing himself as Melvin Parish. A second or two later he sat amongst us, black curly hair, blue and white striped sweatshirt, with a twinkle in his eye and that acceptable smile of devilment. He reminded me of my workmate and mentor 'King' Wright.

On this trip to Burnham river we left Maldon much later on the tide and had a head wind out of Pont, as the fishermen call the Blackwater, which made us late for saving water through the Raysn' Channel. We had two choices, we could either sail out to the Spitway and up the Whittacker or anchor and wait for the tide. Laziness and sunbathing took priority and we dropped anchor. The smack's anchors are all fisherman's patent, some larger than others, we carried four. The largest had very wide spades on the flukes which made it almost useless for holding in the hard sand whereas the second from smallest was sharp and gripped beautifully. Once the flood tide had produced enough water over the ridge which now joins the Buxey to the shore it was not long, running in front of that easterly, before we were brought up in front of the Royal Clubs, where the Rally was to begin.

The programme was for a sail in company the next day up to The Ferry Boat Inn at Fambridge for lunch. This Essex weatherboarded building still has the atmosphere of the marshland watering holes which sailors and the like have known for generations. There are some impressive photographs on the wall of the pub depicting it and neighbouring houses during the Great Flood of 1953, showing the extent the extra water created by the coincidentally freak weather conditions prevailing, that is of equinox tides forced southwards by northerly gales.

On leaving the pub it was to be a race to what is fondly known as the 'quay' at Foulness Island in the River Roach. In reality, it is nothing more than some rough steps up a steep sea wall. Racing in those days did not really include us, for although we had a new mainsail the rest of our wardrobe had little to be desired, coming from wherever we could get it which therefore left it fitting where it touched. Handling vessels in crowded waters, especially ones that you are visiting for the first time, leads to absorbing the options and surroundings on a second to second basis, with the final move made after many options have been calculated and discarded in that short time. This sounds a mess but it is frankly the best way to achieve a fault-free result - the 'mice and men' syndrome. Anyway, being almost last to drop anchor I had more to consider than those who were there first. As we passed the Essex Sailing School's vessel with Mike Tyrell on board, one of my guests apparently asked: "What are we going to do?" To wit I am supposed to have answered: "I don't know yet, I haven't thought that far ahead," and then immediately rounded up behind the next boat and hailed, "Let go". This appealed to Mike's sense of the ridiculous, or so he told me later in the social gathering.

My young cousin Stephen holding the machine gun we found on an aeroplane, out on the "Back of the Main". The vessel was my stern trawler "Notre Dame Des Dunes de Gravelines". The gun was sent to Duxford War Museum.

Foulness is run like a fortress. The MOD use its remoteness and the vast adjoining flat sands to test items designed to blow us all into the next world, as if life is not short enough as it is. For reasons which I believe are called 'Official Secrets' or something, access to the island is very much restricted. However, by kind permission of the MOD, the OGA are allowed on this day to land and be escorted up to The George & Dragon in the village for supper and what have you. The only saving grace of this use of the island is that it has protected the atmosphere of the village from the abomination of bungalowsis. It still has that wholesome feel of Essex marshland proper.

The tide the next day required a choice between an extremely early start to sail the long miles round and through the Spitway or a lie-in to await the half flood necessary to carry us over the ridge and into the Raysn'. I'll give you two guesses which one we employed. This route across the 'Back of the Main' has both advantages and disadvantages. The advantage apart from the later start was the direct course inside the Bachelor Spit, just to seaward of the beacons on the old bombing targets, which cuts the mileage down by seven miles. RAF Bradwell Bay was in use during the second tiff we had with our German cousins. According to my actual cousin, Stephen, who is into that sort of thing, the actor James Stewart made a controlled crash landing in a flying fortress upon those very sands. Is it not funny peculiar that so much effort should be put into aggravating each other, only to be friends later?

The disadvantage is that it is extremely difficult to save the water, let alone the tide to Maldon. Our answer to this was Bradwell Creek, The Green Man's telephone, and a taxi was to repatriate the guests. One, that is Mel Parish, decided to stay for the final leg to Maldon the next day which was fine because we had found him good company. In fact, for two whole days he suffered as target, dupe and vehicle for every joke that floated out of either Barry or me until, near Burnham on the sea wall we saw a man walking with an old-English sheepdog. Mel says: "My brother's trying to get rid of one of those. He had it given to him, the poor thing's only ten months old and it's had six owners already." Far too quick both Barry and myself jumped in, feet first, "Whatever is the matter with it?" With a look on his face that only a victor from the ranks of the oppressed can wear he said, "It can't paint". For those who may not know, there was one of those dogs on a television commercial who used a paint roller.

During the rest of that day in the creek Barry and Mel, at first without my knowledge, discussed the season ahead and the whole matter of liveaboard, sailaways. Later they put a plan to me, which was accepted and in reality it designed our direction. Barry, not of salt-water stock, was hankering after the mountains of Wales; Mel on the other hand, who came from a long line of Humber keelmen, could not believe his luck, having heard what was planned. The idea as put to me was that they should swap roles on board, to allow Barry to

Barry Burton, myself and his girlfriend Caroline in Ostrea's cabin.

return to the land which held more magnetism for him than the creeks and swatchways of Essex.

They both left on a No. 31 bus from Maldon, Barry to his new destiny, Mel to Hull for clothes and equipment so that he could escape from not having a job, which is what he told me.

Barry was always the psychoanalyst of his training, he could not help but identify syndromes and discuss them. He certainly helped me use my grey matter more efficiently or should I say to use it at all. He likened life to being a little fish borne on a solid comfortable rock at the placid end of the stream. Some people are happy to retain that anchor and serve their days in that fashion. Others regard that as living a life of quiet desperation waiting to die. Neither is wrong or right necessarily but should you wish to achieve exploration or the exhilaration of the elusive butterfly you have to have the courage of letting go the security of the rock and its nested comforters to be swept downstream to the possibility of great excitement surrounded by unknown pitfalls. At the time of writing I must admit to having been only somewhere halfway on that journey downstream. Mel on the other hand, at half my age, had the greatest courage where letting that rock go is concerned. It was not until he had been back in

Maldon for over a fortnight that he told me he had, whilst in Hull, resigned his job as a painter, put his own yacht up for sale and told his Mum to expect him when he next arrived but promised to telephone regularly. This same tenacity was to lead him a lot further as we will see later.

The day that Mel returned the Blackwater Sailing Barge Match was being held and I had been down the river with the smack as a spectator. As I moored against the Hythe at Maldon I was confronted with double vision, there on the quay in identical clothes were two Mel Parish's. There was no telling them apart. After getting to know the real Mel as well as I did, his brother still fooled me when he visited our, or should I say Essex Sailing School's, stand at the London Boat Show a couple of years later.

SHOTLEY POINT
(classic boat festival)

The following Thursday we left Maldon just before high water bound down the Wallet for Harwich harbour and Shotley Point marina. The marina occupies a site, once saltings, which became a playing field for HMS Ganges when that training establishment moved ashore from a ship of that name moored in the mouth of the River Stour. She unfortunately, like all the floating training ships, has gone but there are still interesting sights to be seen at anchor in this harbour. From here Nelson sailed against adverse wind conditions, found the Medusa Channel, which he named after the ship he was in, and gained tactical advantage against his target. The lightships once so common around our waterways lay here, brought in by Trinity House service vessels, to be either scrapped, sold off or refitted as automatic stations requiring no crew. Their great red hulls stand out in contrast to the sloping green woodland of Shotley where the square yards of the demonstration mast still stand in the grounds of this redundant naval training school. The 'button boy' was the person at the very top of this rigging whose square yards were manned in true naval tradition by the cadets. At over 140 feet from ground to truck he had only a lightning conductor between his legs to assist his balance on that platform of some 10 inches diameter. I think I'll meet him after he gets down, thanks all the same!

So far in our journeys we have sailed up and down the Blackwater and south through the Raysn' to the Rivers Crouch and Roach. The passage north east, down tide, takes its different course at either the Bar buoy at the true mouth of the River Colne or at the Knoll cardinal buoy marking the entrance to the deep channel of that name, which is bounded by very hard sand shoals. My preference is to take the northerly channel from the Bar buoy leaving the Eagle shoal to the south. Minding only to avoid the hard shoal off the Martello tower near Clacton pier. It is six miles or thereabouts between the piers at Clacton and Walton, which can prove to be the longest six miles in the universe, sometimes even insurmountable in certain wind conditions. The terms down and up, as used by even landsmen who refer to "Up to London" or "Down to Yarmouth", come from the direction of the ebb and flow of the tide. In the Thames Estuary the tide flows along the coast from Yarmouth towards London River past all the rivers in between. It is therefore regarded that the tide is 'up' to London and conversely the ebb is 'down' from it.

Anyway, having fetched a nice quartering breeze from the north west all the way down the Wallet to Walton pier, sailing close to the shingly shoreline, we now leave it to set off along the Naze ledge until we drop into the deeper water of the Medusa. Here we harden in our sheets to point firstly for the Stonebanks, then Pye End, finally passing the breakwater at Harwich. Here you have to stand over more to the shipping channel on the Felixstowe shore to avoid grounding off Harwich - sailing just outside the buoyed channel, which is the yacht track designated by the Harbour Authority. Stretching away ahead of us is the River Orwell whilst to port is the Stour. The marina entrance joins the main channel just in the mouth of the Stour near the confluence of these two pretty inlets. The narrow dredged channel is marked by posts at the outer end and leading marks at the lock gates.

Towing Ian Wilson's Martha II out of Shotley Lock. Many smacks like her have no engine.

We entered the lock and made fast to the cleats on the top of the fender skirt which rises as the vessel and water does. I became conscious of a voice saying: "Good Afternoon, Skipper, Welcome to Shotley". On looking around to see who he was talking to I suddenly realised that it was probably me. In all the time that I have owned boats, since the age of fifteen, I can not recall having ever been addressed as 'skipper'. Maldon fishing boats seemed to have been that way, no named structure as such and yet you knew who was ultimately in charge. We were told that we were one of the first to arrive and that we could pick our own spot at this end of the marina, the far end being reserved for residents.

It was now so hot and sunny that I was concerned for the caulking in the decks. Mel found a hose and turned it on. The water supply to the pontoons at that time was through a plastic type main secured onto the concrete blocks forming the sides of the marina, hundreds of yards of it. Consequently by the time Mel got it, it was like bath water. His remark was: "Blow the decks, I'm going to have a shower", and with that he put the hose on his head. I assumed to do the laundry as well as he did not bother to undress. This larking about was unnecessary when it came to showers and facilities as this marina excelled in that department. The water tower which supplied pressure was built on top of a Martello standing on top of the hill, so it was not so much a shower as a hydro-massage. Mel had a fixation with the whereabouts of baths and showers to the point where I nicknamed him "Hello, I'm Melvin, have you got a bath, Parish".

After scrubbing down, dressing ship and polishing the brass, referred to by Mel as 'happy hour' we settled down to the more serious business of relaxation and meeting people. I think, without doubt, that initial Shotley succeeded in introducing me to more people who have remained friends than any other single event.

The Companie Zanger from Medenblik. Their enthusiasm for singing is insatiable as it is for joining us at Maldon Town Regatta each year.

The first couple of days we did no sailing, preferring instead to socialise and generally soak up the atmosphere. The barge passage race from London River had finished and the majority of the fleet had locked in to join a host of large vessels moored near the entrance. A good contingent of Essex Smacks was also in evidence along with the yachts of the OGA. The element that made this event different and attractive was the evening entertainment in the marquee erected on ground alongside the marina, overlooking Harwich harbour and

Felixstowe. Whilst this was going on Shanty Jack from Immingham was playing musical accompaniment on his squeeze box to those vessels locking in.

So many regattas or boat events are run, certainly on the East Coast, from anchorages or moorings out in creeks. I will be the first one to uphold that that is their natural environment but it is not conducive to social contact in the same way as the original concept of Classic Boat Week at Shotley. Almost for the first time smacksmen, bargemen and yachtsmen crossed the divide because this event was a melting pot with the vessels in close proximity. The organisers had even arranged for the Companie Zanger, a Dutch shanty choir, who sang from the deck of the Sailing Barge *Ethel Ada* during the day and on certain evenings from the stage in the marquee. On about the third day we had a visit from a young chap named Robert who told us that he was mate on *Ethel Ada* and that for reasons of being needed for accommodation and catering the barge was unable to sail at all that week. He went on to say that some of the guest singers were from Poland and would have liked to sail. I asked no more but just said what time can they be ready in the morning. "What about a fee," he said. "No fee, I'm on holiday." "Great, I'll make sure the cook sends a decent hamper."

Time at Shotley was almost immaterial as water to float on was available all the time and the congestion at the lock gates made for the patience of saints. Eventually we were motoring down the entrance channel with our four Polish singers and some friends off another yacht. Robert much to his dismay had to stay with the barge, not that he didn't try to get away. We ran the bowsprit out, set the sails and stopped the motor, which is always a pleasure. You will know what I mean if you have ever worked with an air-cooled Lister - mightily reliable though. The relative silence bred jokes and one liners which unfortunately sparked me off. Poor Mel groaned, "Oh no, not ghosts of Barry".

Although we were joking and tacking towards the Walton Backwaters I felt a little sad that our guests from Poland were unable to join in with us due to their small knowledge of English and with my Polish being a little rusty!! we had a problem. However, music is universal and we all made do with that until one of them who had a little better English than the rest cracked a joke, which only went to prove that England is not the only land of eccentrics.

On returning to our berth in the marina they seemed very concerned that we stay with the boat for the next half hour. We took the hint and did so. In due course they returned and presented us with a Polish flag which they sang to as we hoisted it to the hounds. I was deeply honoured by that gesture.

The recipe contrived at the first Shotley certainly worked, it brought people together, it encouraged fun and gave stage to it. You never knew who you were going to have sailing with you in advance, they would just happen when necessary. I remember once jumping ship in the lock to sail with somebody else leaving mine in the hands of a friend. I must say that he and one other are the only people I have ever left my vessel with in fifteen years but we will meet them later in the story. On the anomaly side again, on fun day - I think the rest of the world refer to it as Wednesday - rowing races, watersports and general mayhem ensued in the lock, along with contests for dogs, rafts and a beauty contest which was won by Den Phillips' brother Glyn. Yes I said brother, he had borrowed a dress, wig, jewellery, makeup - the girls just could not compete.

Wednesday was also rain day, that evening it absolutely tipped it down. The marquee was one of the old-fashioned type with poles in the middle to hold it up. This obviously lead to impromptu racing to see who could reach the top quickest. As I do not have an athletic leaning I took the only course left open to a gentleman and adjourned to the bar. This was a tented annex to the marquee and contained a goodly crowd. Someone made the remark that the canvas roof above our heads seemed to be sagging under the weight of the rain but nobody appeared to take much notice. The rain continued to fall heavily and many more remarks were made, some by those who appeared not to have cared earlier, but still nobody moved. Then suddenly it could take no more and gave way dumping a very large amount of extremely wet stuff all over us - still nobody seemed to mind as the bar appeared to be serviceable.

We decided to join the racing on the Thursday even though we knew that there was absolutely no chance of us gaining a position let alone a place. Mel read the rules and sorted out what we had to do about signing on, start time, and then: "We haven't got a racing flag," he says. "That's no problem, there's a Chandlery here, they're bound to have a piece of bunting." "Right boss, I'll go and see." A few minutes later he returned, "I'd sit down if I were you, No! I'd lie down." "Why?" I hesitated to ask. "They want thirty-five quid," he snorted. "Tain't so likely," I said with my head by this time in a locker, "Here, fly that". "We can't, that's a tea towel," he complained, "So that might be, but that'll fly equally as good as that thirty-five quid." The towel was one

The barge Dawn during her time owned by Gordon Swift. Seen here at the Blackwater Match. Ostrea has her Beam Trawl rigged for eel fishing.

of those ornamental ones you can buy from the RNLI, it had a map of the British Isles with the stations marked on it and their crest in one corner. We rigged it and by the time it was thirty feet above the deck, people were asking if that was our special house flag. I have since that time always flown tea towels, the pattern varying from ducks to knots and the Tetley Tea man. It was whilst flying the latter as a 'bob' at the head of the topmast that a tiny child remarked to his dad, "Look there's the Tetley Tea man," to which dad said, "Don't be silly they wouldn't have that there." Which went to prove to me that the child was observant and dad was blinkered by established mind training. The child then looked at me and said, "Is that a pirate ship?" to which I answered, "Yes, and I'm Peter Pan." Then he says, "If you're Peter Pan, prove it, fly." I was suddenly starting to sympathise with dad's side of the fence as my own smart Alec inner man had just been thoroughly beaten by this miniature smart Alec. Finally, we used to get all sorts of comments from those who managed to recognise the fact that it was a tea towel, like: "I'll bet that makes the wiping up difficult, climbing up there with the dishes."

Maldon bawleys were renown, whilst at the fishing, for the very large clinker pulling skiffs which they always towed. As most of the work was shellfishing and in creeks, loading and unloading made this a necessary system. The same sailing vessel with the same skiff in tow as a cruiser especially somewhere like the Wallet becomes a handful. The skiff begins to surf or snatch, so that you are long stranding the painter which invariably you have already lengthened. This makes the surfing more exaggerated. Then you drop a small drogue in the painter to dampen this, result - speed over ground reduced dramatically. Answer - a pulling boat which will carry five comfortably and safely, has two rowing positions but will sit on deck only using the effort of one man to put it there. A tall order you think? No, we saw one and on returning to Maldon were able to procure same. Taking two days to fit out with ropeways and mast step this GRP dinghy (yes, I am afraid that even I have succumbed), has proven the best all-round tool for the job. It's a nice shape and has won several rowing races at the regattas. Upshot of it was, we moored the big dinghy out of the way in the marina for the week and then nearly went and forgot to take it when we left.

All good things must come to an end and Shotley week is no exception. It can also be said that too much of a good thing is bad for you and people, especially me, were showing signs of being frayed around the edges from burning the candle at both ends whilst trying to heat up the middle. However, I doubt very much if anybody who spent time at those early festivals, will speak of anything less than how great a time it was.

Close quarters at Ipswich.

RIVER DOLPHINS

We sat in the fo'c'sle of *Ostrea Rose*, whilst she sat almost to her waterline in the oozing silt alongside Maldon Quay, pondering on: "How do we follow that?" Several letters had arrived, all of them regarding some regatta or another. We decided to make a forward planner. Was this bureaucracy seeping amongst us to strangle our enthusiasm and freedom in triplicate. What about plans of mice and men? If this was not subduing enough, Mel had to go and mention that desperately boring subject money. We did an audited account of monies in hand and owing, to find that collectively we had £2.82. "What are we going to do for food?" he says. I replied: "I don't know, and that's tomorrow anyway, and I'm not sitting on here wringing my hands worrying about it, I'm going to the pub, we've just enough, coming?" There was no answer but as I went he followed.

On climbing the back steps of The Queen's Head I met Colin Christmas who bought us our first beer and we stood in the 'Sea View' bar initially talking about the video he had taken of us. As we did so a chap put his head around the corner and said: "Just the man, I'd like to charter for the OGA East Coast Race." "Not a problem," I replied: "Would a deposit of £50 be alright". The deal having been struck I turned to Mel gave him £20 and said: "There, my little worrier, food money." We passed the rest of the evening in pleasant conversation ending up back on the smack for coffee. Colin is an accomplished architect with as far as I could see everything going for him. His parting statement that evening has stayed with me, "Well, I'm going to hate you two tomorrow." "Why?" "Because you two have it cracked." Did he realise that only five hours earlier we did not know where the next meal was coming from. Or does that matter? Some long while later Colin came into Maldon and announced: "I've taken your example, I've retired."

The days that followed saw us as maintenance men and fitters. We painted the bulwarks, cappings, coamings and put an extra coat of varnish on the brightwork. It was at this time that the pulling boat was fitted out, with the large old skiff being pensioned off to become a junk store for all those pieces of equipment you keep because, "they're handy if you never need them".

The middle of July has since the early sixties been the time for the OGA East Coast Race. The early races I understand were to be passage races to Harwich but I was too young to be involved at that time. My first race was to be with John Bray in the *Nell*. We did not do very well as I remember but attended the prize-giving anyway, which was held in the Yachtsman's Arms at Brightlingsea. The following year the Stone Yacht Club played hosts for the race day, which is where it has been held every year until now, that is at the time of writing. Apparently this year we are to visit the West Mersea Yacht Club. The first year it was held at the Stone I raced my own smack *Happy Days* which I had just purchased, I was fifteen. I drop this in just to show that I was young once, honest.

(Overleaf) John Bray's "Nell" with the author at the helm during the 1966 Old Gaffers Race.

(Below) Happy days with Peter nets hanging up to dry.

True to form on the day of the race we were practically the last vessel to turn up, and finding somewhere to let go the anchor was looking nearly impossible, with a fleet of almost a hundred vessels in attendance. Mel flaked the chain and made the anchor ready whilst I picked a spot I thought I could get her to bring up in. The plan was to stem the ebb, getting as close to the stern of the big Tollesbury smack *Charlotte Ellen* as possible, let go and trust that it bit to stop us from driving back on the yacht downstream of us. Should this have looked likely my escape route was to motor ahead, shear out into the deeper channel and retrieve the anchor as we went. Anyway, it was going to plan, we were slowly steering our way towards the *Charlotte Ellen* when Mel suddenly went crazy on the foredeck, before I had chance to even consider what I had got wrong a large body rose out of the water, with an eye that appeared to be looking directly at me. The shock value was absolute to the point where I did nearly collided with the *Charlotte Ellen* missing her

only narrowly after I had collected my thoughts and sense of concentration.

We finally anchored and the liberty boat delivered our day charterers. They also told us that two dolphins were swimming in the area. Having seen one of the creatures myself I thought it rather dark in colour. On the television films they are a grey/blue sort of shade, the one I saw leaned more to being almost black. I remembered the old hands talking about the shoals of porpoises that came to the Thames in times before the war and wondered whether the liberty-boat coxswain had it wrong. It is marvellous what does swim in the Blackwater. I caught a sizeable salmon just off the promenade at Maldon in 1969 and at the time of writing the river regularly has seals, one having visited Maldon several times just before Christmas. Also, a whale, pilot I think, was kept alive by buckets of water and guidance when the tide arrived back sometime around 1972. The knight errant was the landlord of the pub at the Stone, Robert Lovell, who was assisted by a chap we called "Dave the Grave" because he was always digging holes in the beach looking for lobworms. This noble deed was pictured in the *Daily Telegraph.*

The Salmon pictured here in the Queens Head. Tony Frostick, with whom I part owned the "Olive", was the spirit of the true wildfowler. He made several punt guns.

The race itself I am afraid passes my memory totally but I am sure that we must have circumnavigated the Wallet Spitway as normal. Back at the anchorage though I remember being fascinated by the fact that these creatures of the deep were so sociable. They visited boats and lingered but only if they were inhabited. As soon as the occupants either took the liberty-boat or rowed ashore in their own dinghy, the watery visitor passed to the next available vessel with life on board. Eventually, it was our turn to be shore party and we made for the Yacht Club. I got talking to someone whom, I don't rightly remember now but he said that an expert had been dispatched to monitor the movements and behaviour of these creatures, which had been positively identified as dolphins. I remarked about the colouring and was offered the argument that a bit like chameleons they take on the colour of the water in which they swim.

In Maldon, I was very lucky to have the use of shower facilities at a friend's house in Church Street. Laurie and Ava Wood were all suffering and extremely kind but Ava used to treat nearly everything I told her with a sack full of salt as if I was constantly pulling her leg. As if I would!

So you can imagine the reception I got when I told her about 'dolphins in the Blackwater'. Certainly one remark was: "You've spent too long in the Queen's Head, again." My just desert was to be served, and I did not have to wait long. Only a couple of days later Laurie and Ava, who were both architects, had chartered the sailing barge *Reminder* to take out some of their clients. The skipper Bob Wells lived actually next door to them in Church Street. His house saw births, marriages, deaths, parties and all manner of family comings and goings related to mine covering a period of over one hundred years. I digress, the morning dawned so fine that it looked like a watercolour painting. We motored, as did *Reminder* down to about the North Doubles. We then set the sails but it was the strong ebb that drove us eastward, as the canvas hung lifeless. This did at least allow inter-boat conversation, which inevitably came round to Blackwater dolphins. Ava still convincing herself that I was telling tall stories started to put me on the spot, as it were, with her guests as the twelve men just and true. I looked at Bob, who I knew had the knowledge of these creatures, he merely smiled and said nothing. Then Ava says: "Well, where are they?" By this time we had drifted more or less level with the anchorage at the Stone and I pointed in the general direction and said "They were over there ......". I did not have time to say any more because one rose out of the water almost where I was pointing. What a result, I do believe there's a tooth fairy after all. This was not to be my last encounter with the dolphin. In mid August there is smack racing every day for a week, except Wednesday (half-day closing for smacks, or something) at West Mersea. I was asked by several boats who were going if I would take my big clinker-built pulling boat to use as a ferry. Although the ferry service is superb there - one, they get swamped during the rush hour and two, nobody wants to miss the last one home, without a survival kit to fall back on. So I took it.

The racing starts about 0900hrs at the WMYC line near the Nass Beacon at the entrance to the Quarters, apart from Saturday which always seems to be one hour later and is run, I am told, by the Town Regatta rather than Mersea Week. As I have said before racing in those days did not really include us and we gathered names like Posteria Rose and The Sailing Hearse but never mind we did not care for it's not the taking part that counts it's the bally winning, all right! Sorry got a bit carried away. We were generally first in the clubhouse though. That diesel and its large propeller did have its uses. As a lot of the smacks today are kept almost purely to race, a good proportion of them have no engine at all and therefore no ballast problems or propeller drag. This is fine whilst the wind and tide serve but is a real barrier to progress when it does not. I remember leaving Maldon one early morning, the sun rising over a glass sea, with the cobwebs in the rigging promising an easterly by around lunchtime, bound away for a race that was destined to start at the Nass. By the time I rounded Mêtes Hard to look down the Basin Reach I had two smacks to starboard, one to port and two in tow behind. They all went on to beat us in the race. There is a compromise to be drawn if that is at all possible, which I doubt, as there is never a good one between winning races and windward performance or being able to almost guarantee the return of your paying guests to their cars and structured life. Sailing vessels in the days of commercial sail spent the most part of their time at anchor awaiting a fair slant, unfortunately this nine to five world does not allow for that, more is the pity. If it did I would be the first to remove my "infernal" combustion motor.

My little bald headed smack towing its large pulling boat.

Once the racing was finished we motored past the Old Oyster Packing Shed on its island and on up to the creek where we moored fore and aft to some piles. From here it's a short pull through the 'cut' to the hard, which now sports a floating pontoon leading to the Coast Road by the Fishermen's Refrigeration Plant. It was whilst making one of my frequent ferry trips, sometimes with as many as a dozen people on board, that I made acquaintance with the dolphin for the last time. We were within feet of the hammer head in less than four feet of water when the children on the platform started shouting and jumping up and down. I looked round to see the dolphin pass between us and the excited little ones on the pontoon. A while later it, or both, were sighted in London River which was where we were bound so we had hoped to see it again, but alas it was not to be. Reports had it that that year a porpoise had stranded right above Maldon in Heybridge Creek. The local river bailiff also had to deal with a porpoise carcass that had washed up on the saltings to the north side of Osea Island. I do not know what attracts them, or for that matter what drives them away, but can only comment by saying that that summer had been a real good one weatherwise.

Before we leave West Mersea there is a tale of fate, luck, coincidence, call it what you will. Poor 'owd Melvin had toothache. Unlike plastered broken limbs it does not attract sympathy in the same way, not until your face looks like it's growing another on the side of it. He blew up like a balloon and needed treatment. There was obviously going to be a snag here, for it was not only Saturday lunchtime but also Mersea Town Regatta. The whole island's involved in this but when needs must and all that, we rowed to the pontoon at the hard. To say there were hundreds of people would be an understatement. What we needed was some local knowledge and I could not see any one at all that I knew from Mersea. So I scanned the crowd, saw a likely looking character and said that we needed a doctor or preferably a dentist. She replied by saying: "Go to the end of the hard and wait, I have a car and will give you a lift." I said that was very kind and she answered: "That's no problem, I'm the dental nurse."

"Abscess" makes the heart grow fonder.

UP SWIN TO LONDON RIVER

We returned to the Hythe at Maldon once Mersea week had subsided and started our preparations for a trip to the great metropolis. A place where according to Bob Roberts, erstwhile owner and master of the last sailing barge to trade, people sit in brick-built holes and pass each other pieces of paper. Whilst Bill Linnet, the punt gunner from Bradwell, blamed the use of electric light instead of oil lamps and candles on the fact that many people now have to wear glasses. Undaunted, we were prepared to do as Daniel did and go into the lion's den. Mel had met a young lady named Gayle Pawson whilst we were at Shotley and she along with a chap named Jullian Ballantyne were to accompany us 'Up Swin to London'. When we first met Gayle the conversation from our side seemed to consist of a lot of references to television programmes, which was of little consequence to her as she lived in a house that had never suffered with one. On asking her what she did without the attention of the animated fishbowl, her reply of constructive, positive and enlightening pastimes made me feel, to say the least, a second-class citizen. Her example has led me almost directly from that time not to own one and I have seen very little only at other people's houses now and again. Her father, Des, whilst in conversation with me at Shotley, was debating the pros and cons of taking the plunge into making his hobby a business. He was into fancy-knot tying, fenders, bell ropes, that sort of thing. I can at the time of writing say that Des and his wife have a well-established firm named Footrope Knots, and his articles appear regularly in the traditional boat press.

The other great character we met through them was a gentleman who said he had owned the same vessel for over fifty years and had always done his own maintenance and alterations. We had a guided tour of this 26 foot Broads sailorman which took over an hour, with not a minute of hesitation or boredom. I asked if he was staying for the whole week, expecting this very elderly but sprightly looking gentleman to say, yes, because I am retired, but far from it. He announced that he had to return to work on the Tuesday, also he felt it unfair to leave his wife as she was no longer able to get out much and missed her sailing, which they had always done together. I started to feel sorry for the old lady and considered sorrowfully the disadvantages of old age, when he cut in and said that the reason for her being house bound was because she had to look after his mother.

As I had never been right up London river to Tower Bridge, we had to look for charts to give us some idea of distance and probable obstacles. The only one I possessed was one bestowed upon me when I was fifteen years of age by Alf Claydon. He was like a Grandad to me and we had some good times together both on the water and off. As we poured over this Stanfords Thames Estuary chart, the first thing that struck me was the variation at 10°50'W, of late I knew it was in the region of 4° W. This led us into searching for the date and there it was, 1934, with not one correction. If all this was not bad enough I noticed the only land objects marked for the mariner were the asylums. Were the cartographers trying to tell us something? "We'll have to have a new one, blow the expense," I said, and set off for Dan Webb and Feesey which proudly advertises in its window Admiralty Chart Agent. I am afraid that led me to mislead myself as to what I was going to find once I had passed through the door. You see John Bray, with whom I used to sail in *Nell*, a 16 ton yacht built on Falmouth Quay Punt Lines, had been a chart agent for J D Potters in the Minories, London. When I visited him there (that is *circa* 1967), one could purchase off the shelf a chart or pilot book for just about everywhere in the world. It was an amazing place, the surroundings and atmosphere were straight out of a Charles Dickens novel. I entered DW&F, they did indeed sell charts and in fact had some on display but not unfortunately in the quantity I held in my vision and of course the one I wanted was not amongst them, so back to 1934. I worked on the premise that London must have remained roughly in the same place and therefore the geography would be close. So assisted by an up-to-date East Coast Rivers book, and some local knowledge, at least as far as the Whittacker, we decided, not that we had much choice, to proceed.

In any passage to London River it is advantageous to pick up the first of the flood somewhere about the South Whitaker buoy or certainly that side of the Spitway. This cross tide swatch bearing S23°W magnetic (1996) from Clacton Pier, has in its lifetime moved, or at least the constantly changing sands which govern it have. In 1934 the bearing of the buoyed channel was S14°E or put in the notation more widely used then, S by E 1/4 E. Thus the usable channel has moved its position in a south westerly direction by some two and a half miles and contains only five feet of water at ordinary springs. Coincidentally this is found to be the same in its 1934 position, moreover in Frank Cowper's book, Sailing Tours published in 1892 he remarks about there being only five feet in those days. He went on to suggest that due to the direction of the ebb and flow in the Thames estuary the cross tidal swatches would eventually silt right up. Leaving, he said, the passenger steamers that visit Clacton pier to pass around the north east of the Gunfleet or take the only channel that would be left open to them, the Rays'n. In his day, apparently, the Rays'n was deep enough to be of use, if a little narrow. However, his assumption that it would survive, whilst the Spitway disappeared, has been proven wrong for the head of that channel now shows a drying height, sadly.

Bearing in mind the distance from Maldon to the 'new' Wallet Spitway and given a fair wind, which we had, it meant we would be there long before the ebb had finished. So we let go the anchor at Weymarks and had breakfast, pulled the dinghy on deck and generally tidied up. We got underweigh again and were reaching down the Knoll Channel. Behind us and closing rapidly in the dark was a tall gaff rig vessel. She passed us as we were going through the Spitway and disappeared towards the Whitaker. We carried our sails until somewhere near the Blacktail Spit, where it was becoming obvious that the wind was straight down the river. Our objective was Gravesend to anchor and the only sure way for us to make it before the ebb came down was to motor. By the time we were level with the Chapman Sands we had caught up with the big vessel that had passed us in the night. We identified her now it was daylight as the A.D.C. She was still sailing topsail and all but was unable to achieve the same windward performance as our 'iron topsail'.

That evening I was on a trip down memory lane, for the last time I visited Gravesend was now nearly twenty years distant. They say you should never go back because of disillusionment. Things then were always bigger, grander, brighter and far more acceptable, or so the memory will have it. My last voyage there was in *Nell* and unfortunately for her, at the grand old age of 98, she passed away in a fire, or as we would rather remember the sad occasion, a Viking funeral. I sat on deck and viewed the shore but for some reason could not locate the buildings of the Old Shrimp Brand Brewery. My grandfather used to freight their products around in sailing barges to the Essex hostelries. It was the first clue as to why you should not tread the actuality of memory lane. It had gone, replaced by some ghastly flats. Not taking notice of the signs I was keen to row ashore and visit the Canal Tavern. When John and I used this watering hole all those years before it was a proper four ale bar with pictures of steamers and sailing ships, brass fittings and a beautiful model of Everad's barge the *Greenhithe*. Its clients were watermen and tugmen, the talk was of ships and London river. Oh dear, what a shock, I did not recognise the place, the building was just about in the same spot and that's all you can say about it. I was devastated. We went in search of the yacht club which according to our written instructions was playing host. This they did handsomely. The atmosphere was pleasant and friendly and at least here one felt unaffected by the brash transparency of the modernised world that was creeping like a relentless tide across a sandflat.

Unloading a beer barge at Fullbridge Wharf Maldon.

The reason why we were here was a race from Gravesend to a line comfortably downstream of Tower Bridge. It was a follow on, so to speak, of the races in commercial days when hatch boats took oysters to London and sold them from the deck of the vessel at Billingsgate. Re-enactment races from the Horse Bridge at Whitstable had been run in previous years, with baskets of native oysters and porters on hand with their special load-carrying hats to complete the scene. Sadly old Billingsgate had gone, replaced on the Isle of Dogs, by a clinical, tiled, transport unit. Coincidence seems to play a great

(2nd Photo) Promotion photograph produced for the authors firm Maldon Oyster Fishery. Showing open "deep-cups" as well as No. 4's through to "Royals". These were known as Ware oysters to distinguish them from immature stock, which were known as spat, brood and the halfware as they grew.

part in my life, and the old sayings like 'That which goes around, comes around' hail true time and again. The last native oysters I sold were to an agent on Billingsgate during the final week at its old site. This firm, Bloomfields, was amongst half a dozen or so which I had served in London. My biggest customer was Wheeler Restaurants in Lisle Street, behind the Talk Of The Town and it was they who were running this race.

I think I have already mentioned that I had never been in the reaches between Gravesend and Tower Bridge so the plan was to have a dry run. Gayle had, for reasons I cannot remember, to leave before the day of the race. As there is no suitable overland route from Tilbury to Ipswich without going to London it seemed like killing two birds with one stone for us to reconnoitre the eddies and tide rips, then deliver her to Tower Hill. I remember being told by the old hands, that the use of the tide rips and set was as constructive as trying to sail. Having now experienced these I appreciate what they meant, even if we did not get it right all the time. Eventually we came upon the bridge that I was amazed to find had only been opened in 1894. For all the world it looks as if it was built in a much earlier period.

We searched almost in vain to find a landing stage upon which to set Gayle. The only place that looked even likely was a dumb barge moored in-between the entrance to St Katherine's Dock and the bridge. We decided to give that a go and made towards it. It was on nearing the sides of this rusty hulk that I realised Mother Thames is never still. The waves and wash caused by water taxis and passenger boats is relentless. Once it had reached the edges it rebounded towards the middle to mix it up with the fresh lot just created. The dumb barge consequently was rising and falling quite violently. Our first pass was good enough, Gayle jumped, bags were thrown, hasty goodbyes made and we made a sharp evacuation, watching the mast against the bridge as we turned. We dropped back to our now familiar anchorage at Gravesend for what turned out to be yet another pleasant evening in the Yacht Club as crews of other smacks had by this time arrived.

They say familiarity breeds contempt or a least a lack of concentration, the night before we had left the skiff on an anchor after calculating the amount of rise of tide coinciding with our return from the Club. It was almost spot on. The second evening you would have thought that our calculation would have been even better as we were by this time almost locals. I fear not, for when we arrived back, admittedly a wee bit later, even though we had pulled her further on than the previous time, she had the appearance of being almost out in mid stream. A few yards looks like miles when all you have to get you there is a pair of thigh boots. Whilst Jullian and myself deliberated over the possibilities, like spending the night on the park benches, Mel stripped off, dived in and swam out to the boat. On his return he mumbled something like: "You'll not catch me sleeping on the beach when there's a comfortable bed just out there."

Alongside Dick Harmans "Electron" in St. Katherine's Dock, London, under the shadow of the Ivory House.

The next morning, race instructions and token oyster baskets were issued. We found that Jullian could read and do joined up writing, so he was nominated to be tactician. His first order was that we had to be dressed as 'authentic dredgermen'. Piece of cake I thought, diving down the after compartment and fishing out old great coats, leather jerkins, flat caps, thigh boots and hessian sacks to wear hung from a line tied around the waist. They were on board from the time of her being at work dredging in the Blackwater and me being a jackdaw, were still there.

If you think we looked out of place dressed like this on the Thames at Gravesend, you should have seen us at the Dickens Inn, when we arrived at St Katherine's. We looked as if we belonged to the era in which the building first saw the light of day, whilst its regular clientele so obviously belonged to the modern city world, with sharp suits, brief-cases and mobile phones. The conversation seemed to me to be in some sort of Enigma code. APR, MLR, BMW and so on. I suppose if I'm honest our conversation would have seemed equally in code to them with things like, let go in two fathoms, a couple of cables south of the ..... and so on. Anyway, I was not the only one who felt it, Dick Harman of the smack *Electron* said to me, "What do think of it," I said, "That's alright," to which he replied, "Yes, that ain't for the likes of us". I was a little disappointed in the result of the fancy dress which went to some chaps in polo neck sweaters and bobble hats, the judge obviously had never been afloat in a smack at work. I doubt that it was our theatrical prowess, more the boat itself that won us a picture spot on page three of the *Daily Telegraph*. It was taken on the start line from, more or less, head on with the large Faversham smack *Gamecock* crossing behind us.

It was to be a head wind and light to bout all the way, consequently the little narrow smacks were in their element, pulling away with every board they put in. We and the heavy boats were soon left to make our own entertainment. A bawley named *Mollie*, which I had owned and fished with some years earlier, had been rerigged and was our constant companion for the duration. Sailing in the upper reaches is a most frustrating business, for the wind if not completely fair, is constantly on your head or appears to be, then it will come down a street or worse over a building. Either shaking the gear or laying the boat down but only temporarily whilst in that small vicinity. We always make friends wherever we put into with the boat and London was not to be any different. For instance we met the crew of a smack I had never heard of before called *Valkerie*, perhaps named after the big yacht of the same name? She joined the fleet from a different direction to everyone else, by lowering her mast in a tabernacle and passing under the bridges. She had come from as far west as Eel Pie Island where her owner had a boatyard. Another acquaintance struck up in the bar resulted in an extra crew member in the form of Dave Brown for the trip back to Maldon.

We locked out just before high water the next day and did not consider canvass at all but instead opened up the turbine to clock off as many miles seaward as we could manage before the tide was done. We hoped, rather in vain I'm afraid, that when we reached around Gravesend and some clear water we would be able to set the gear up and make a fetch with the northerly prevailing. As with northerlies in the summer it died with the sun but this one was to have a sting in its tail. We motored on and made an anchorage in Hole Haven, home years ago to the Whitebait boats. It seemed only polite, whilst there to hop over the wall and have a pint of the landlord's foaming broth in the Lobster Smack Inn.

We entered a not particularly crowded downstairs bar and were waiting to be served when a gent, whom I did not know from Adam, looked at me and said: "How's the fishing, still making a living?" Admittedly, I was wearing a blue Guernsey. Apart from that I was in clothes any one would wear, so was this another coincidence because how else could he have known?

We set the clock for just before 0300hrs, it went off and I turned out. I went on deck to find my dead northerly blowing a good five

gusting six. I think had I been anywhere else I would have gone straight back to bed but Hole Haven does not hold much in the way of romance for me. So without further ado we slipped and motored out into the young ebb tide. It was reasonable until we reached Shoebury where the wind over tide kicked up a rather nasty swell but luckily it was dead head on. I took the time on a mark and then another some-while later which showed that despite heading into this horrible sea, she was making a good seven knots over the ground. This cheered me up because at this rate our passage would be fast and therefore short. As there was no point in everybody suffering on deck, Jullian joined me and left the other two in their pits.

Just before daylight Mel put his head out of the hatch and asked if we wanted some tea. I told him that it would be very welcome, also that we would set the gear at the Wallet Spitway buoy to fetch up the river. The reply, typical of him, was: "Right-oh boss, don't whip me!" By the time he had made the tea, dawn had started to break, down to eastward. The wind was still strong but somehow had lost its vicious feel, whilst the sky all round was black and heavy with a light line at sea level towards the north east, which was widening as the sun rose. Mel appeared on deck with the cups in a bowl to take up the spillage and said: "I'll get the jib ready and chuck off the gaskets." I was fixed on that light sky which was getting bigger than ever. I replied: "Don't bother, there ain't going to be a breath time we're through the Spitway." "What!" he says, "It's blowing hard." "Look at that sky," I replied. "You're a blooming old fraud, you, I'm going to set it." He did and it drew us to just the river side of the Knoll before the wind went completely and the sun warmed the morning as only a summer sun can.

With this respite from jumping about, attention turned to breakfast. Jullian volunteered to be chef and disappeared below, replaced by Dave on deck. He seemed to be down that hatch for an inordinate amount of time. Thinking he had fallen asleep I went to investigate. I found him sitting on the little sea chest we use as the cook's seat looking, to say the least, embarrassed. "I can't get the plates out of the cupboard", he said quietly. "You're not the only one to have been caught by that. The centre door does not open, so you take the right-hand bowls out and roll the plates sideways. It's easy," I related. "That is what's so embarrassing about it." "What is?" "I'm a cabinet maker by trade." Well, it had been a long night.

The rest of that trip was a pleasant sunny sail up a very welcoming river to Maldon and our berth on the mud.

(Opposite page) Jullian Ballantyne keeping the oyster dredges company after the wind dropped.

HIGH WATER AT LONDON BRIDGE
HALF TIDE IN THE SWIN
LOW WATER IN YARMOUTH ROADS
HALF FLOOD AT LYNN

A Polish friend Chris Vorbrich with his boat "Orion V" at Tower Bridge

SCOUTS, OYSTERS AND FAMILY

So far we have been either racing or to a regatta but sailing does not consist of merely these pastimes. There is cruising and exploring the inlets and creeks whilst soaking up the beautiful surroundings of the Essex marshes, so much maligned and regarded by modern people as waste ground. It holds many fascinations, much history and to me more magnetism than any mountain range, however high or snow covered.

I remember working with Ray Payne, gathering winkles on Bullen Beach which bounds Joyces Farm, when from one field a startled flock of Brent geese rose, counted in their hundreds and making a deafening noise. They circled, calmed and returned to their grazing. I wonder how many people in the course of their employment are 'paid' in such a manner. The VDU screen in the enclosed office under fluorescent strip lighting may pay pounds sterling better than a longshoreman can achieve, but no money, which is let's face it an abstract commodity, can buy that kind of wealth. There are so many payments of this kind if you are not in a rush for reimbursement. Seals in quantity on the Maplin edge of the Crouch or the odd one who visits you at anchor, peering at you as if he is a watery David Attenborough making a documentary on the habits of humans.

I have only once seen an otter and that was on the saltings at Mundon Stone Point but mullet using the tuck of the smack as a parasol were a regular occurrence, being viewed from the taffrail above like a giant aquarium. Much wildfowl visit especially during the winter, bringing migrants, stragglers and oddities. We once had a flamingo swimming with the herd of swans that live above the

Fullbridge at Maldon. Opinion had it that it had probably escaped from a zoo and certainly that is where it ended up, if indeed in a different one.

The swan herd adopt and embrace other species with a great deal more ease than I would have given them credit for. For a long period, up until their disappearance, two white domestic geese swam with them. The geese, who I suppose were used to people, encouraged the swans to actually knock on the side of the boat. Whilst sitting on the rail became a precarious business with the long neck of the swan being able to reach up and give you a peck to draw your attention. This attention was, I must add, probably due to our feeding them. I use 'our' in the wider sense because everybody treated them as pets. The two geese were even named, they became Gert and Daisy.

Mother with her brood, she raised them nearly all, losing only one.

Ducks were also visitors but not until the shooting season was over. During this period you would be lucky to catch a glimpse of them at great distance, whereas as soon as the shrapnel stopped flying they became equally tame. It's almost like they ticked off a calendar. I awoke one morning in the late Spring to the sound of quacking and a deep thud, followed by a drumming noise. I gazed upward from my bunk to the flat perspex skylight above me and there for my entertainment was the undercarriage of a dancing duck. The bird had landed on the hatch, which being wet with a heavy dew (or dag to give it its proper Essex terminology) gave it no traction. It was like Bambi on ice.

Even the lowly gull can be of interest, the little terns roost on the water, such that if you are bound away in the early hours on a calm night, the Basin Reach can be full. As you motor along they lift in waves in front of you, but not until you are right on them, and then only the next few feet of them, the rest awaiting your imminent arrival before they then lift and so on. At this point I am reminded of Barry who said in front of an ornithological group: "A mate of mine used to throw stones at them," which I thought was an insensitive, rather provocative thing to say, in fact one woman was about to launch herself into the argument of man's inhumanity towards his fellow living creatures when Barry said: "Yep, he didn't like to see any tern unstoned." He couldn't help it, you know!

In-between races or charters Mel and I would commute between Maldon and Bradwell on *Ostrea Rose* for what became known fondly as the 'post run'. My mail at that time was still delivered there, so periodically we went to collect it. On the particular day in question spontaneity let go the ropes and before a few minutes were past we were congratulating ourselves on awarding this beautiful day and fair wind to the two most deserving characters we knew. Gybo! at Bradwell Spit beacon a short fetch up the creek, leave the green buoy to starboard, knock the jib out of her and pick up the bobstay. Down main but just leave me some peak, half down staysail work out the weigh, right down all and fish up the tail on the mooring buoy. Brilliant, everything has its place and a place for everything.

Drop down below, kettle on, then suddenly the bottom dropped out of our world. As I reached for the coffee jar I realised what our larder reminded me of, it was Old Mother Hubbard's. "Melvin", I shouted. "Yes'um boss." "We've got to do some shopping," I announced. "Well we've got to go ashore, there is a shop here isn't there?" "Yes, but one - it's Wednesday and they're shut, and two - how much money have you got?" It was another one of the major audit times by the liquidation accountants, it was pitiful and I was hungry. "What are we going to do this time, oh one who doesn't worry?" I must admit I was stumped because we could not even eat at the pub without money. "I'll buy you breakfast at the cafe in Maldon as soon as we get back and I have been to the bank, how's that," I pleaded in mitigation. "That sounds like a top plan for tomorrow, but I'm starving now." We sat on deck wondering what on earth we had sailed ourselves into and as we did so I watched the birds feeding along the edge and the mullet swirling the water as they turned back and forth. "Come on," I said with a start, "We'll go and get a net from the house, I'm sure there's still one old monofilament net in the shed that will catch some of those mullet." "Oh yea, I've heard it all now," came the retort. "No, I'm serious but we'll have to hurry before the tide is done."

We ran up the road past The Green Man, went through the shed like a couple of bulls in a china shop and were soon returning to the skiff with a fifty yard stop net and two buoyed anchors. Mel rowed the skiff along the edge of the creek whilst I tied the first anchor on. We saw a fish turn: "That'll do, turn and pull across the gut." I threw the buoy clear and dropped the anchor. I then payed the net straight out of the bag as I did not think I had time to overhaul it into the sternsheets. As it happened it went out clear and before I had chance to bend on the second anchor we saw a fish strike in the netting causing a sizeable splash at the surface. I started to haul because there was no point in catching more than we wanted but before we had retrieved the whole length two more were gilled in.

Our total catch was three, one just over 3lb and two something under double that. We gave the two large ones to the neighbour of the house and set to preparing the small one to eat. We borrowed some fennel from a garden and I gutted, headed and descaled the forthcoming gastronomic delight. Some people argue that they are not nice to eat or that they are muddy to the taste. Frankly, I think the English palate has been used to cod, plaice and haddock for so long that they have become acceptable over other more exotic species out of habit more than anything. Also the argument of the muddy, or strong, taste is due to the fish not being properly cleaned. I was in discussion at one time with somebody about the eating and cooking of mullet and they forwarded a recipe to deal with them. They said what you need is an engineering brick, preferably a hard blue, and some tin foil. You lay the fish on the brick, cover it completely with the foil and bake it for six hours in a red-hot oven. You then unwrap it, throw the tin foil and the mullet away and eat the brick. Honestly, there are some Philistines about. I think mullet are tasteful, we certainly enjoyed that one, even though its flavour may have been enhanced by necessity. Whilst rummaging through the shed, Mel found the remnants of a square sail which I had cut up to make a spitfire jib. "What's the chances of having some of this, then boss?" "Help yourself, but what do you want with that?" "I'm going to make a smock." He did, but the dressing, old catachu and fish oil kept leaching, especially when damp. It was so stiff that it would stand unaided and threatening in the corner of the cabin.

Whilst at Bradwell on one occasion we attended to the garden at the house, or should I say rainforest that had engulfed the surrounding land. We hacked down just about everything we came across and had a bonfire Samuel Pepys would have been proud to chronicle. Like the Phoenix that garden rose from the ashes in a few days and looked a picture, despite us. We left Bradwell, as we thought, knights amongst gardeners. On our return the story was oh so different, it was as if we had never touched it. The saying my old companion King used to hold forth came ringing in my head: "Set concrete seeds and paint it green." He was a keen gardener as you can tell.

The next time we visited Bradwell it was to rendezvous with some chaps from the Loughton and Epping area. The trip had been arranged by Alec Burrows. I had met Alec in The Jolly Sailor. He was an acquaintance of Ann, who was at that time Barry's girlfriend, 'wheels within wheels, like a circle in a spiral'. To cut a long story even longer, Ann had been encouraging him to go sailing and was suggesting *Ostrea Rose* for the purpose. Now, Alec was a man of many parts, fitter than most men you have ever met, let alone the over fifties, as he was. He played football at aggressive level, climbed mountains, hit everything that required a racquet and had a smile that you would recognise at a mile distant. He had also been, in times past, a very active scout leader and the chaps we were to meet were those boy scouts, except this was now twenty years on, since their time in the 4th Epping group.

Alec Burrows and the Author.

I heard a car pull into the drive and looked out of the window. It was an immaculate black BMW, top of the range looking vehicle. The door knocker resounded on the outer door and I went to open it. Standing in front of me were two very well dressed men of about thirty-five years of age. Looking for all the world like city bankers or barristers. "Good morning, we are part of the Alec Burrow's group." "Come in," I beckoned. "We will fetch our bags from the car. Perhaps you would be kind enough to allow us a room in which to change." I showed them upstairs to one of the bedrooms and went back to the living room. "What have we got here this time," says Mel "This looks like a right barrel of laughs, stuffed shirts if you ask me." I was just about to say keep your voice down, they'll hear you, when they appeared through the door. The sight will never leave me, you needed sun glasses on to look at them. Bermuda shorts, trainers and the loudest shirts you have ever seen, topped by those ski glasses you can buy. "Where's the action boys?" was the opening shot. I looked at Mel and said "I think we are going to need a bigger barrel".

I nicknamed Alec's groups the 'sardine run' because to make the trip economic on both sides we doubled up on bunks, slept on the floor and even in the sail store aft. Whilst all necessary codes of practice were observed and the wide decks served to spread the passengers beyond anyone feeling crowded, there is only so much room below in which to fit berths, especially when you have a large engine room like *Ostrea Rose*. Having said this we always seemed to manage happily.

In the cooking department, I learned a great deal from those lads about supplying high quantity, acceptable quality, hot food, using the scantiest amount of equipment. I have been congratulated many times upon my serving breakfast to large crews and can say that it is all down to what I learnt from Alec's boys.

As you might imagine the humour stemmed from cub camp days, with in-house jokes and one liners surviving the ravages of the years to still find their target just as they had all that time ago. Alec is, being as kind as possible, a bit thin in the hair department. This lead to one or another almost constantly pretending to polish his head, or the question might come: "Would you like a cup of tea with a head of hair on it, Alec?" Another, in-house joke, about which I asked was why they kept calling Alec, Betty. Apparently Paul Simon had made a record with the line: "I'll call you Betty, you can call me Al", and it had stuck. This type of wisecrack went on almost non stop.

Following dinner the next evening we were like Ali Baba and his forty thieves, bundled and packed into 'our den', the smack's cabin. "Who am I?" came the question. "Are you dead or alive?" We were into a who's-who twenty questions game. Several of us had a go. I remember being Stonewall Jackson, whilst others were Winston Churchill, John Wayne and the like. Then it was Alec's turn, question

Melvin, on the bowsprit, was asked by his father, who was skippering Strata IV, to slow down so that he could take this photo.

after question pinned down all the facts except the actual name. He was a footballer, English, alive as far as we knew, well known Alec said, and lots of other details. In the end we conceded defeat, awarded Alec the point and asked who he was. He came out with a name like Fred Heplethwaite to wit we all said who on earth is he. "He played centre half for Epping Town when I was a boy." "Oh come on, Alec, we thought you said he was famous." "He was to us, proper hero, he was." Alec disappeared under a barrage of hurled hats and other assorted missiles.

During all this mirth and merriment the lads were actually, genuinely, trying to sail the boat and learn about it. All this time I have referred to the group as lads but in fact there was a young lady in our midst. She was, by comparison, extremely quiet and did not appear to get involved much. Towards the afternoon of the second day she asked if she might have a go steering. I was at the helm at the time holding it with a tiller line. I let it go, passed her the rope, and stood to one side. The smack, as will happen with all long boom boats, wound herself almost instantly up towards the wind. The young lady put the line around the tiller from underneath which is correct to obtain the best purchase. She pulled the tiller towards her, whilst looking aloft at the bob. The boat started to draw her weigh and we were sailing. It was a confident, correct manoeuvre well executed and I must say here that I had not seen any of the lads at quite this standard. "How long have you been sailing?" I asked. "Since Saturday morning," she replied. "No, no, not on here, I mean in general." "Since Saturday morning," she reiterated, "I've never sailed before." "Well if you haven't you're sure making a good impression of knowing how to do it," I remarked. "I've been watching you teaching them and how you put them right, when something wasn't and thought I might give it a go." Every now and again you get a natural borne to an activity of some sort and she certainly looked natural to sailing.

It was like living in a whirlwind being with those chaps but come Monday morning at a quiet Hythe in Maldon, we missed them.

In any summer season you hardly had to blink before there was another event to attend, only this time it was two. On the Saturday it was Colne Smack and Barge Race and on Sunday the Oyster Dredging Race at the Colchester Oyster Fishery. Fate again, for in my earlier days I had served that company with both full ware and brood oysters but had not seen Christopher Kerison, its managing director, for some years so I was looking forward to that. I now had a problem, an oyster dredging race means that the participating vessel has to be equipped with the said implements and I had sold mine. The man I sold them and other equipment to was a watch and clock repairer from Chelmsford, Chris Papworth. A strange place and customer to which my redundant gear should go, you might think, but Chris had just rebuilt Peter Vince's old boat from West Mersea and was a keen weekend fisherman working from Bradwell. I rang him up to ask if I might borrow the dredges for the weekend, explaining why they were wanted, and he kindly lent them to me. He even delivered them to the Hythe, which alleviated the transport problem.

By this time I was without a motorcar, having taken the conscious decision to do without. You see, living on a boat and ending up in different places, sometimes being forced to go somewhere other than the original plan (not often, luckily), meant that the car was always somewhere else and required public transport or taxi's to retrieve it. It soon became obvious that it was cheaper and a lot less hassle to simply use public transport. The only consideration was the need for better forward thinking regarding your travelling timescale. The benefits at journey's end were that you had no need to find a parking space, which seemed always to be at a premium both in terms of space and cost. Whereas the railway and omnibus companies look after their own toys as soon as you have finished playing with them. At the time of writing I have just celebrated my eighth anniversary without a car, whilst the car industry is celebrating the 100th anniversary of its development. Personally, I think mankind would have been much better off had it never been thought of.

All passages under canvas are a pleasure, but journeys which are simple, easy sailing, and result in trouble-free quick arrivals do not leave much to say about them. I suppose that's why the majority of books and stories about ships and the sea always seem to be high winds, disaster, shipwreck, fog, foul gear and broken this and that. Makes you wonder why we do it. Anyway, we had a totally enjoyable, trouble-free sail to Brightlingsea, where we moored alongside the trawlers on the posts opposite the hard. Should you ever go to Brightlingsea and find yourself on that hard you will notice to the right of it as you walk to the waters edge, the remains of a sailing barge. It was one of the barges my grandfather used to haul that beer in from Gravesend, her name was *Khardomah*.

The pub overlooking the extensive hard is The Anchor and is a most unusual building. It always puts me in mind of the sort of building that might be used for the set of some Walt Disney ghost of a pirate film. The inside, however, is more like those large, late

Caroline Eagles's Medway Bawley 'Thistle' followed by Hyacinth, showing the difference of rig between her and a smack.

Victorian London pubs. As we rowed ashore I noticed a bawley I had not known previously, she was called *Thistle* and was of impressive proportions. During the evening I was introduced to her owner, a rather slight, elegant lady named Caroline. She was, at that time, rather unique in the smack world for precious few females even wanted to sail in such vessels let alone like her, own one. The situation as at the time of writing, I am pleased to say, has altered somewhat but that is for later in our story. I remember being impressed by her knowledge of the Medway bawley and of her total allegiance to that type over and above the others. Her interest went beyond the vessel for yachting purposes and she wanted to know the vagaries of a sailing vessel at work. I told her about Sunday's event and suggested that the best way to understand it was to actually do it. She agreed and we made arrangements to meet first thing Sunday morning.

The race on Saturday, as its name implies, included both smacks and barges. It is a superb sight for anyone who is interested in working sailing vessels. Where else, certainly in this country, could you behold such a spectacle, fifteen or sixteen lofty spritsail barges jockeying for position off Bateman's Tower, whilst the same amount of smacks and bawleys wend their way clear in that narrow channel. What a sight, but a sobering one too, for under the gaze of Bateman's leaning folly we are witnessing what is left. Active sailing barges now probably number less than forty as opposed to the four thousand or so recorded before the Great War which diminished to nine hundred recorded by the PLA in 1938.

My old friend King only recently related a tale about the time he was in the Stack Barge *Dawn* with 'Hobby' Keeble bound for London. They got underweigh that morning from Harwich along with fifty-two others and another time from Shore End in Burnham river with thirty-seven. The *Dawn* had been built in the last years of Victoria's reign by Walter Cook & Son for that part of my family ancestry which were farm merchants. My grandfather had been brought up by Hesakia Keeble and was apprenticed to Walter Cook as a shipwright. Family legend has it that not long into this apprenticeship, the grandfather Rowland Emmett was put in the saw pit. Large timbers were cut by a double-handed vertical stroke saw by two men, one at the top and one in the pit getting covered in sawdust. This did not seem to be to the grandfather's liking because he apparently told Walter that if he had to take his jacket off to do a job, it was not worth him doing it. Much later he appears in Brentford, Middlesex, as the owner of a builders and undertakers business.

In the summer of 1995 I was sitting on deck alongside the Hythe when a man in his sixties asked if my name was Emmett. He then told me that he was a Keeble from Brentford, and was the grandson of Hesakia and that he was compiling a family tree. What he then related is an amazing story of bad fortune. Apparently, during one year all that time ago, the Keebles, who were a huge family in the true Victorian style, had lost two brothers drowned out of barges, and one lost in a deep-sea square rigger. This tragedy lead Hesakia's wife to persuade him that barging was too dangerous a way to make a living and that he should become a greengrocer. He took the advice and they moved to Brentford, where he opened a shop and had a 'round'. If barging appeared to be a dangerous profession, greengrocery was to prove even more fatal because poor old Hesakia got run over by his own horse and cart and my grandfather buried him.

The race down the Colne changes course at the Bar buoy setting then towards a temporary mark laid near Clacton pier. From here we set away from the land towards the clanging bell of the Wallet Spitway buoy. With the last mark being the Bar left to starboard we look towards the gap between Point Clear and Mersea Stone for the finish line to be exactly where we started. The prize giving was always held on the steps of the Colne Yacht Club and with no formal gathering planned splits into small groups in various hostelries or private cabin parties. We thought we would start in the club and see where that might lead us. This establishment has the finest collection of Lloyds Registers I have ever come across and the barman kindly let me have the key to the cabinet, so that I might have a look at them. These documented 'yachts', so I knew that looking for the barges or smacks owned by the family in times past was of no value. However, my father had owned a vessel named *Topsy* which I knew had been built originally on a site next door to the very club we were in by the original firm of Robert Aldous in 1911 as a yacht. She, long before my father bought her in 1939, had been cut in half and lengthened by twelve feet as well as having her rig altered. Here I thought was something worth looking up. I started by identifying her later state, working backwards through the years, as these books are published annually. I reached 1921 where it records all the alterations and the name of the owner at that time. I put the book down on the coffee table where we were sitting and then noticed the rogues gallery of past commodores and was interested to see that the man who had all this work done to the boat was in that same year commodore of the club.

I was to find out more the following morning because one of our charterers came from Heybridge Basin and remembered her there as a houseboat. For some years we were under the impression she had been taken to Scotland because that is what her owner at that time had told us he intended to do. According to our charterer she went no further than the Walton Backwaters when she left the Basin. A further snippet of information came from Jimmy Lawrence, the sailmaker at Brightlingsea, who told me an old lady had offered him, at one time, some gear which she said had come out of *Topsy* and although he did not take up the purchase he did remember that she came from Kirby le Soken. Maybe *Topsy*'s bones lay quietly in the mud around that way somewhere. I have for a long while said that a reconnaissance trip to find her might be an interesting thing to do, on the other hand would what we find be a sad sight.

On Sunday morning having collected our full complement for the day, or so we thought, we motored out of Brightlingsea Creek and across the Colne towards Pyefleet, where the Breton style building of the Colchester Oyster Fishery nestles behind the sea wall at North Farm, with oyster pits and a hard made from oyster shell mixed with shram that leads to the edge dry of the creek. It was here on the hard that I made my reacquaintance with Christopher Kerison, he stood there in White Star trawlerman's boots. If I had not seen him for a long while it had been a great deal longer since I had seen a pair of those. We shook hands and he said: "It's good to see you, I'm glad you have been able to come, it's nice to see those who dredged oysters for a living, there are not many left." I'm not sure quite how this fact or compliment, if that is what it was, left me feeling. Anyway, we collected our instructions and rowed back aboard to move our position to another mooring nearer to the mouth of Pyefleet.

Christopher had devised a whole new concept in handicapping, which is always a nightmare and a bone of contention - outside class racing yachts. The idea was that each boat, depending upon how he had perceived its ability in previously watched racing, was to be positioned on moorings gradually reaching further up the creek, so that the fastest vessel had the mooring furthest in, to which they had to return as their finish line. On top of this there was a time elapse for each boat to start under sail from that mooring designated by Christopher arriving in a motorboat and shouting BANG because the gun had jammed. Oh, I nearly forgot you have to pick the buoy up under sail as well, in order to be within the rules.

The course once out of Pyefleet leads briefly up the Colne, taking the early flood with us, turning then into Geedon Creek which circumnavigates Rat Island. "The kind of time that sorts the men out from the boys." Short tacking in shallow water creates a situation

The powerful Leigh Bawley Bona in close confines during the Colchester Oyster Fishery Race.

(Top pic)
Oyster Dredging.
(Bottom pic)
Emptying cultch from a hand dredge.

where if somebody does ground, the rest have the pleasure of trying to get past her. Back out into the river again towards Fingringhoe, a red can to starboard and we're off down the Colne to the designated dredging ground on the Point Clear side of the channel, just to seaward of where Brightlingsea Creek runs in. As the rest of the crew sailed the boat, I bent the warps and buoys onto our half-dozen dredges, sorted out the tholepins for the rail and arranged the dip pail and sheards, with which we were to dispose of the cultch overboard. We made our station pulled two reefs down but only tying just enough of the points to hold up the loose canvas. Changing the large jib for the Number 2, we tacked leaving the jib sheets made fast but lowering the halyard somewhere about halfway. Let down the staysail completely and chucked one dredge after another, 'ring to tide' to ensure they reached the bottom the right way up. We only needed one oyster for the rules of the race and first pull up produced three, "Right-oh, get them others but leave the forward most one till last, we'll spin round on that one." We hoisted the staysail and shook the reefs out, changed the jib back up again and were off to the mark which was level with the Molliette Beacon off on the Bench Head. So far we had held our own against the others in short tacking in the narrow confines, done well in the dredging, as far as I could see but then just when we did not need it, some clear water windward work. With our propeller creating a scene in the water resembling an agitated washing machine, I think we lost a good half knot of forward performance, enhancing our leeway by 10° or more. Still with Christopher's revolutionary handicap system, we did at least have the fleet of greyhounds in sight when we finally hove to and fore reached onto the mooring.

Long before *Ostrea Rose* was built I had bought for me as a Christmas present, a Queen Stove. These are very ornate, with shutter doors and a flap grate, resplendent in black lead. When given it I made the comment: "That's lovely, we'll have to build a boat around it," not realising at the time that many a true word is spoken in jest. 'Howsumever', as the 'owd hands' used to say, we lit it that evening because the autumn air was by now cooling down and in comparison rather than reality we felt chilly. After a short while the 'very effective' little stove was being very effective and nobody below could stand it. In the end we were all up on deck sitting around the column of hot air that was coming out of the hatch above the stove.

The full complement for that day, of which I spoke, was to include Alf Hodgings, but he was nowhere to be seen and as time was pressing

Smacks trawling. Boadicea, originally built in Maldon in 1808, led by the Mersea "Mayflower", once owned by Bob Stoker.

we had had to leave. Little did I know at the time, poor old Alf was the victim of the first world war example of messages being passed down the line, where, send reinforcements we're going to advance, became send three and four pence we're going to a dance. In Alf's case he had 'phoned my mother who told him that the race was at Pyefleet and that he was not to be late. She omitted to tell him that we were actually based at Brightlingsea for the weekend. He then used his commonsense and assumed that we were racing on Saturday, because races were always on Saturday, except this one. Taking my mother's instructions to the letter not to be late he had arrived at Mersea Stone at 6.30am Saturday morning, whereas we were basing our intentions on the reality of wanting to see him about 7.30pm Sunday at Brightlingsea. The first I knew of this monumental lack of co-ordination was when Richard Titchener of *Sallie* hollered out: "I've got a present for you." It was Alf. Apparently and thankfully Richard had taken pity having come across him on the beach in those early hours of Saturday morning. Alf's compensation was that he had been able to race in *Sallie* for the Colne match.

FROM TOLLESBURY TO THE SOLENT

From the late Victorian era, up to the outbreak of the second world war, that was to end so many institutions and ways of life, Tollesbury fishermen and professional yacht hands had manned the finest yachts in the world. By comparison today Tollesbury is a quiet backwater. A marina has now replaced the yard where dozens of smacks fitted out for the winter fishery and famous yachts laid up.

The only visible clue left is the sail lofts which overlook the mud berths out on the vast saltings that stretch away towards Mersea Island. Having said the only visible clue, that's not quite true for in the Sailing Club are pictures and photographs which record the great yachts and the men who sailed them. It is from here with the generosity of a business man and smack owner, John Rigby, who supplies the beer and a buffet, that Tollesbury Smack Race is run. I like Tollesbury, in fact the clubhouse is one of the most homely I have been in, but from a logistical point of view it must be the worst place to try and visit by boat from Maldon. The high water times are within a few minutes of each other, whilst the distance apart, taking into consideration rounding the Nass must be a good ten miles with both being half-tide ports. The only slight advantage Tollesbury has over Maldon is a floating anchorage called the 'Leavings'. Here you may stay afloat, well just! but you can only leave once the tide has flowed for an hour or so. Also the channel is narrow with a dog leg in it.

(Opposite page) Richard Titcheners Sallie turning to windward with the Barges during the start of Colne Match. Picture by Dympna Veaney.

Advantage, I called it, because the nearest you can comfortably anchor like this to Maldon is only just above the Doubles buoys which must be at least two and a half to three miles downstream. However, after you pick your way up the hard, which resembles stepping stones, the walk around the sea wall is approximately a mile to the club and the village itself nearly the same distance again up the road. For all this we still make the effort.

The club asked me on one occasion if I would be one of their winter speakers, which I accepted. As we (and this will be explained later) live on board and have no road transport it seemed logical to us to sail down from Maldon, drop the boat in the leavings, pull the skiff up to the wall, leave her on a long painter and make the walk around the wall to the club. As it was raining a little and muddy underfoot we wore oilskin frocks and thigh boots for the hike. Once at the club people were remarking about us arriving in what they seemed to think such a novel fashion, especially considering the time of year. Whereas we had regarded the choice a bit like a snail does, where I go so does my home.

This race, like others, started at the Nass, then looks up river to Thirslet buoy, which due to bureaucrats and committees no longer has any relationship to the use and position of the old "Thuslet beacon". This at least did have a physical relationship to the vast shingle and mud flat that bears that name, whereas the green pole buoy of today is getting towards being in mid channel. Whilst I am having a little moan how about the colour green, what a choice, especially over black which the buoys used to be. The old fishermen used to tar their fishing floats, for even in the dark it is the best colour to stand out against the water, whereas green is the colour of the water. You can see Thirslet when you're practically on top of it though, so rounding it was not too much of a problem.

Standing then towards the north shore to cheat the flood tide for the run back down to the West Mersea course No. 3 racing buoy. Leaving that to starboard that is if you have not been lured too close to the shore too soon. From Mell Creek, where Tollesbury pier used to stand, you can sail the cant edge all the way to the No. 3, which is level with the end of the sea wall where it becomes the long mud spit of the Nass. Above this point a flat ground protrudes towards the mouth of Thirslet Creek which has much less water over it and starts with a high shingle spit created by Mell Creek's entrance to the river. Several vessels, none that will be named, the Gentleman in me precludes me from divulging such information, have been left here

Afternoon chat in Tollesbury.

awaiting the tide. The course is then seaward leaning now towards the south shore, to again try and cheat that stubborn flood. As we become visible to St. Cedd and his chapel, which he built in the seventh century, we are able to see our seaward objective, the Bench Head. This single marker is not only the outer limit of the Blackwater estuary but also used in conjunction with the Bar buoy it is the entrance to the River Colne, whilst used with the NW Knoll it bounds the channel of that name. From here it is homeward bound for a finish line at the Nass but it does not stop there. Sighting the dinghy which has been left on an anchor in the quarters, the canvas is shortened to more handy proportions and you creep forereaching towards it. With the long boat hook you catch the painter as far away from the skiff as possible, one hauls the anchor whilst another takes the weight of the boat finally making her fast to the taff-rail. Bearing away and letting the bowline go the smack starts to draw along the South Channel towards the leavings. On this occasion we have been invited to take a berth in the marina so we enter Woodrolfe Creek to sail past 'Rotten Row', as the fishermen used to call the moorings that lined the saltings, then pass over the sill that maintains the water in the marina on the ebb, to moor alongside Nick Moseley's *Fly*. Here the rest of the afternoon was spent in pleasant conversation whilst sitting in the sun.

A packed club house watched the prize giving and we stayed only until the tide, which waits for no man, forced us to remove the smack from the marina. We could not stay overnight because we were destined back at Maldon on the next day tide and I have already explained the problems of that. The plan was to drop back out into the Leavings and wait there until the morning. Once we were looking down that waterway, I could see a straight passage over the spit which had plenty of water on it because of the time of the tide and the wind was set for a beam fetch to the Bradwell shore. That would save us the journey around the Nass later I thought so we set the gear up and stopped the motor. We sounded with a long pole, just in case, but carried reasonable depth over it until it dropped off the edge into the deep water. For some reason I then held her as high to the wind as she would have it and we made a board, looking considerably above Bradwell.

On reaching the south shore Mel asked where we were going to anchor and rather than answer straightaway I put the idea of a night sail to our charterers. They thought about it and decided it would be interesting, so we tacked for the first of what was to be many boards during that dark passage. Bearing in mind that it was a foul wind and a foul tide being challenged by an under-rigged, beamy, shallow-draft bawley dragging a huge propeller, it may have been, on the face of the facts, that our choice was stupid. Also bearing in mind the old adage that: "Gentlemen never go to windward." However, the wind was increasing, she was plainly winning and I was having a good time.

Richard Sibley second from right and friends.

We made ground on every board, especially now that it was blowing something like a reef breeze and we were carrying the lot. It proved one thing that night, beamy vessels like *Ostrea Rose* will carry far more canvas for longer, than a narrower vessel is capable of. The only place where we nearly got beaten back by the tide was in the narrow channel between the Black Bar and Stansgate Shoal, at the eastern end of Osea Island. Several times we were aware that if we had not lost ground we certainly had not made any. Then suddenly we seem to break free and forged ahead at least twenty yards on one board, which then became more until we were able to gain a couple of good tacks, using the 'Doctor' mud for cover. "When are we going to anchor, ain't you had enough, you're mad, you," came the vote of confidence from my foredeck crew who was as always content with his lot!! "Leave the bo'line on, knock the jib out of her and pick up the bobstay," I replied as I put the tiller down and we wended coming immediately hove-to. "Let go," I hailed forward and turned to Richard who stood beside me, "Right, we'll have that main." Following a quick tidy round, we landed the skiff on deck to prevent her banging against the smack and were down below for a cup of tea and a warm bunk. "Where are we," says Mel. "Off the mouth of Cooper's Creek," says I, to which he said, "And where the hell's that?"

I told him that we were downstream a little way from Southey Spit, which he knew, but he said that he wanted to see this creek we were in the mouth of because he had not seen it before. I said no more and turned in. I was awoken by Mel saying: "Well, where is it?" I put my head out of the hatch and pointed to a tiny rivulet running off the mud. "That's it?" he said, with disgust in his tone. "Afraid so," was all I could manage, "like most of the creeks around here that one has silted up almost to nothing."

Charlie Stock and Shoal Waters.

I was to sail with Richard Sibley again, not on that occasion in my vessel but in his. We travelled down to the Isle of Wight where he kept a small open gaff cutter at Bembridge. It was to be my first sail whilst it was daylight in the Solent, I had been out of the Solent from Southampton bound for Brittany on a previous occasion but that was in the dark. On the Saturday morning we walked down to the creek, where the beautiful, colonial style Bembridge Yacht Club stands, home of the famous

Redwings. One of which Lt. Col. Moore-Brabazon fitted with an aeroplane propeller or more correctly termed a gyro rig. This worked apart from the lack of suitable braking facility. I was told, that on one occasion it apparently would have wiped out the fleet as they lay on their moorings had it not been for some quick action on behalf of the waterman.

Ironsides at Cowes

As we reached the beach I was confronted with a familiar sight, there sitting on the sand was *Shoal Waters* with Charlie Stock waiting for his kettle to boil. "Morning," he said as if he had expected me to be there. We chatted for a while, during which time he told me that he had been on the Norfolk Broads earlier and had recently returned from the Dunkirk veterans, gathering. This may not seem adventurous in the grand scheme of things but what one has to consider is that Shoal Waters is little more than a class sailing dinghy with a cabin on it. Well designed, I might add, but still small for bashing about the North Sea. Charlie has for over thirty years sailed just about every piece of navigable water there is, from the North Sea to the canals and inlets as far as to where they became culvert pipes. I am almost sure that one day I will turn on the tap to see Charlie tacking up the drip.

Our mini cruise was to take us to Cowes and up the River Medina to the Folley Inn which I am sad to say was shut. I am still to visit this hostelry, for my next trip some while later on the River Medina also resulted in our bypassing the establishment. I saw it that time from the deck of a sailing barge, called *Ironsides*, which I had helped Adrian Mulville deliver from Maldon to Newport for a firm called Topsail Charters.

The nights are as good as the days, if not better

TRANSPORTATION AND DEPARTURE

The last race of the season, at that time, was the Osea Race. Run from the Island, with a start line off its now dilapidated pier - in reality probably half of it no longer exists - with the outer end long gone. This once sported a small building and a cast-iron lamppost upon which the light to navigation was put. The race is for classic yachts and smacks which turn up in great numbers to this invitation-only event. The prize giving and gathering afterwards was held in a barn by permission of the owners of the island, Mr and Mrs Cole. The smack racing was co-ordinated by the owner of *Sallie*, Richard Titchener, who one way or another was responsible for, or was perpetrator, be it directly or indirectly of, the ladies only team in that vessel. Whatever, or however, they are now a formidable team. Whilst Roderick Kalberra, owner of a West Solent, amongst others, co-ordinated the yacht racing. The course was out of the river to a mark and back again. Sorry, the memory stays with me of what a spectacle all those boats made but the race details???

Osea Pier.

Osea Island has a history and associated stories about naval boats and inebriates homes all of which are documented handsomely in other authors' works, so here I am not going to reiterate them but are to return to my childhood when we used to visit the island by boat and how I found it the most enchanting place. The type of haunt one expected to find Arthur Ransome in.

It was here, after summary conviction, that my grandmother's goat was sent for penal servitude. My grandmother and her second husband Clem Last owned a tea-room on Maldon promenade. It originally served the charabanc trade which brought the Cockneys on their day out to the seaside. As late as 1969 it was still serving large numbers who arrived, by this time, in motor coaches. Seated at long tables they feasted with 'silver', as the cutlery was referred to. This had to be laboriously cleaned once a week in addition to the customary washing. These long tables were covered with proper tablecloths, dozens of them, all of which had to be washed in a copper every day, put through one of the two giant cast-iron mangles and hung out on linen lines to dry in the summer sun. These lines were in a field next to the café and the grass used to grow profusely. In fact, it grew a lot faster than peoples enthusiasm to cut it down. Consequently the staff started to complain about wet feet and damp stockings from the early morning dag as they pegged this washing out. Then some bright spark had an idea why not buy a goat, that would keep the grass down.

No sooner thought of, it was done. Cilla, as this goat was christened, was bought from Chelmsford Livestock Market and put to work the moment she arrived. Everybody was happy, no more grass cutting or wet feet. However, it was not long before the moaning started again. This time the staff were complaining about being head-butted, and generally harassed by Cilla, who by this time had eaten most of the grass and had taken a fancy to the linen, even that being worn by the women. Something had to be done, it was decided that Cilla could have a go at the grass in the orchard at the back of the café. This was up so high that pygmies could have lived in it undetected. All went well, till someone noticed that the trees were suffering. Cilla was debarking them. She had to go, the ranch was not big enough for her appetite. Cecil Wright, a relation by virtue of my grandmother's marriage, had a vessel called *Rosenna* and a friendship with the farmer on the island at that time. He agreed to have her, so she was loaded on board Cecil's boat and transported, in the best penal sense, to Osea Island. A happy end you might think, well not quite. A little while later I met one of the hands from the island and asked about Cilla to which he said: "Don't mention the word goat to the guvnor, the thing's nearly eaten the island."

The end of an error (as an old friend of mine from Norfolk was once heard to say).

On the trips that followed we started to wear jackets and boiler suits even in the middle of the day, the places we visited were noticeably quieter and the nights were cool enough to search out those extra blankets. Orion was standing once again in the sky and the threat of winter loomed. We, after trying to ignore its onset, finally discussed the possibilities for this period of short days, fog or gales and persistent damp periods. The options open, I must say, were not many and such as they were it was becoming obvious that they would not support the team as we had come to know it. I announced that Mel should not consider me, as I had ridden out worse, than what looked to be on the agenda this time. To which he said that he thought he could lodge with his mother in Hull and get some work with his old firm. And so the man that came for the weekend and stayed seven months was gone.

Towards the end of the winter, about February I think, a telephone message came that Mel had rung. I contacted him and the voice at the other end said: "Hello, boss, what's doing for the summer?" "Nothing concrete that I know of yet, but that's as usual," I replied. "It's just that I've been offered a job on a square rigger," he continued, to which I immediately said: "What an opportunity, go for it," following a second or two of silence, he asked, "I need a reference, what's the chances, buddy, old pal?" "That'll be in the post, just let me know how you get on."

I sat down and thought about this reference business and drew, to start with, a bit of a blank, for I had neither received nor given one before. Then I remembered my father's papers which were amongst the photograph albums. I could recall them as being references he carried from one naval ship to another as his command changed, back in the dark days of WW2. Having searched them out I picked one, they were all much the same, typical Admiralty. Nelson I think would have recognised the wording. I entered Melvin Parish and current dates where necessary and sent it off on some headed paper that I had formed using Electroset lettering and my old smack logo from the oyster company days. He told me later that he had got the job but it left me wondering about the recipient looking at that document scratching his head and thinking who on earth has he been working for.

LAST OF THE SAILING FERRYMEN

Once again a bit of a void to fill, though the situation was nowhere near so severe as the previous one, for this time it was merely what to do with the future available rather than; I'm on the scrap-heap of the past. However, short-term economics were a consideration becoming daily more pressing. I had to find business or gainful employment because reserves were bordering on 'spring ebb'. Also a man has to have a reason for getting up in the morning and right then I could not even find a decent book to read, I was bored. I took my boredom for a walk to see if Maldon promenade was still where I had left it. The Spring was just starting to show nicely in the sky, around the hedgerows and upon the Hythe, where the bargemen were fitting out. I sauntered in that direction and then stood looking out across the river. "Fancy a cup of tea," I heard. It was a chap I had met maybe only once previously, named Ray Payne. "Sounds like a plan," I replied, and walked the gangway to board the sailing barge *Vigilant*. During our conversation he told me that he was fitting out the barge for her owners Martin and Judith Daws but was falling very behind. He then said: "What are you up to?" to which I had to admit, "Frankly, not a lot." Then came, what appeared to be the answer to my problems: "If the owner agrees, do you want to give me a hand?"

The following day I was replacing the servings on the standing rigging where necessary and dressing the wires with boiled linseed oil. Over the days to come we received the sails from the sailmaker's store, they were heavy Royal Navy flax, and we dressed them with what passes for ochre these days. The owners used to arrive weekends and assist in the work. In fact, in one weekend, they lowered down, rigged and hove the gear back up again. This left us with jobs such as painting the barge boat and generally touching-in round the fittings on the gear, which were painted white. It was during these last days that I made the acquaintance again of two chaps who had chartered the *Ostrea Rose* the previous year. They were both in the fence and gate business. One of them, Bob Wright, has become a friend in general. Though that's a wonder, because I nicknamed him 'Bob the fence'. After a while he said to me, jokingly I think: "Look, this 'the fence' business will have to stop, I'm getting people offering me dodgy gear." Anyway, they wanted to sail, so we arranged a suitable day and Ray volunteered to come as mate.

Ray Payne.

The smack was on the old Bath Wall fishing boat berths, where she laid on her port bilge, when the tide was out, with her gear swung out to ensure she always leaned that way. We boarded and tied the skiff alongside. I then slid the forward engine room hatch off and dropped down below. "Ray, can you chuck those decompression levers in, if I swing her," I asked. "You've got all mod cons on here then," came the reply which made me consider her equipment. The water I kept in stone jars and breakers, the lighting was two wick lamps and heating was a coal fire. The only modernisation that has occurred from the smack's equipment of my childhood was the calor gas cooker, which has an oven. This was a vast improvement on the old pump-up primus, with its pricker and meths bowl, that we used to use. I was, in time to come, given some batteries and had electric starting fitted on the motor. This gave rise to a chap called Mike McCarthy making the statement: "He's been dragged, kicking and screaming, into the 19th century." When I said: "Don't you mean the 20th," he said: "No, I think I was correct the first time."

I tied the forward pair of mooring warps to the after pair with a light line and secured a buoy to it. We then let go the forward, upstream pair and pulled the after, off mooring along the port side. The result was she sheared off stern first, turning as the flood tide caught the heel leaving us pointing towards the oncoming tide, over which we motored until just round Metes Hard. We then set the gear up and gradually crept towards Osea with a breeze that was far from strong. Bob asked if it was possible to go the north side of the island and as it was now nearly high water I could not see any problem with that. We fetched over the causeway with about seven to eight feet on it dropping then into 'Stumble' and away towards the mouth of 'Earl'. It reminded me of the many times I had made these manoeuvres and passages when we used to be winkle gathering on the vast muds 'over Stumble'. This time, however, we were to be film stars, Steve had a camcorder and wanted to get some footage of the boat underweigh. Bob assured me he could row so we cast them adrift and sailed round and round until Steve reckoned he had filmed enough.

Then off we went to Brightlingsea but the wind failed before we arrived, so we had to motor up the Colne and into the creek. We dined ashore at The Anchor that evening on victuals like you would expect at home for a price so reasonable that we could not understand how they made a profit. To top that the lady came out when we were nearly finished and asked if we would like seconds.

Unfortunately Bob and Steve had business commitments the next day and ordered a taxi which left Ray and I to sail the boat home. Bob has got involved with rowing more seriously since then by buying a scull with a sliding seat and scoop-bladed oars.

During the sail down the river the conversation got around to why some smacks have topmasts and some do not. Well it's all to do with balance and what was expected of the rig, work wise. In *Ostrea Rose*'s case it's rather more simple than that. She lost hers whilst she lay alongside a wharf on one occasion. A crane swung round catching hold of the topmast shrouds which then snapped the spar like a carrot. So she became a bald-headed rig, if a little under rigged. Having considered this for a while Bob announced that he might be able to obtain a suitable tree through his contacts in the fencing world. Some weeks later a lorry arrived with four trees. "I didn't know which one you'd like best, so I've fetched them all," says Bob. "I'll have to pick one then." "No, they're all yours," he says. "How much do I owe you?" I worried. "Nothing, the bloke owes me a favour." We landed them on chocks in the yard at Bradwell where I was shortly to hue out the smacks new topmast.

I was telling a friend of mine, Sam Rothwell, of my good fortune with the trees and that I would have to go to the house at Bradwell sometime to fashion it up. "If we can be back tomorrow evening I'll come with you, I'd like to see that house, anyway," she said. "Alright, we'll go this tide, we can have dinner at The Green Man." It did not leave all that amount of time in which to adze down and plane up the spar, clear up the yard and load it aboard, before we had to be returning to Maldon. I think I must have sweated blood but it was completed, only leaving the furniture to be fitted later. Sam was a friend in the platonic sense to the point where we decided we must have been closely related in a previous life, which gave rise to her being regarded as my 'sister' and on at least one supportive occasion I could not have wished for a better relative.

Adzing down the spar.

The new topmast was much longer than the old one, which was fine where the standing rigging was concerned because it fitted better than it had the old one. Unfortunately that was not the case where the old topsail was concerned. A bargeman and beer connoisseur, Kevin Murphy, elected to help me stitch what can only be called bits and pieces onto the ageing ill-fitting topsail. We pushed and pulled it about until it seemed to fit but somehow not quite. Then it started: "Headstick, that's what it wants," says Kevin. I should have seen the signs. Do you know if Kevin had had his way the smack would have been sprit rigged. As it is I have rigging that owes its evolution more to freight barges than fishing boats. Having said this it works a treat and I am indebted to Kevin for his help.

We were to sail and discuss, make lists of alterations and execute them for several weeks to come, for Kevin and his girlfriend, Vicky, lived on the smack due to bargework being a bit thin. He used to refer to her as his 'colonial', owing to her Canadian background. Our first trip with the patchwork topsail did not have a destination as such but the course to nowhere held us fairly tight to the north shore of the Blackwater in a down river direction. Sailing very fast up the south shore, was a smack I did not recognise. Even through binoculars no one on board could identify her. When we returned to Maldon we remarked to Nick Moseley who owns *Fly* about this vessel. He told us that it was Ian Wilson's newly-rebuilt *Martha II* on her first time out and that he and everybody on board were wondering who the tall rigged smack was on the north shore. When we attended the second

Headstick topsail designed by Kevin.

Kevin steering Ostrea Rose chased by Sallie.

Colchester Oyster Fishery race Christopher Kerison's words were "Michael, you've sprouted a topmast and confused my handicap system". It became plain enough to both Kevin and myself that we had made and adjusted all the spars and rigging that seemed possible. It was now hand in pocket time for the sails to hang on them, a daunting financial proposition.

It was in this year, just before Kevin and Vicky moved on board, that I had my most bizarre charter. I was sitting on deck having a cup of coffee when a gentleman approached me and asked if there was a ferry across the Thames. He went on to tell me that he was from a family up north who had been into manufacturing, fairly well since the industrial revolution and that he had inherited the business. He then said that owning that sort of business in this day and age was a nightmare so he had sold out, which had given him time to do what he wanted. This seemed to be a cycling holiday, the like of I had never heard. With his American girlfriend they had followed the minor road systems all the way from his home in the north until they had met the Thames corridor, where motorways and tunnels seemed to be the only alternative to London. These, I can understand, are not attractive to cyclists. As they looked at their road map they saw a ferry marked at Southend and had been there to find it non-existent.

Up-to-date maps, I thought, for I remember as a child going on the *Royal Daffodil* and *Royal Sovereign* from the end of the pier but they had not run for many a long year.

The story then expanded, because he said that once they had got across the Thames they were going to cycle around Europe. Crossing then to America where they intended to cycle across to California and on to the young lady's home town. It wore me out thinking about it. Then he says: "Would you take us across the Thames?" My immediate reaction was, "It will cost you more than it's really worth, because of our speed and the distance, also I'll have to have a mate." "Try me," he asked. So I quoted a reasonable price but one I personally thought he would turn down, instead of which he said: "When can we leave?" I looked at the tide table and said: "About midnight." "Great, I'll bring the bikes and our gear down."

A little while later he and the lady arrived with a pair of cycles, which carried their entire life and were, to put it mildly, state of the art. I had never seen so many gears and so much equipment, working off the moving parts of the machine. They must have cost a fortune and this started to concern me, for they would not fit down below. The best alternative was to lash them inside the starboard rigging and to the bulwark. Seemingly ready, I still needed a mate and was flicking through the files in my head as to who I could get at such short notice, when Ray Payne appeared. "Fancy a trip to Queenborough tonight," I more or less pleaded. "When are we likely to get back?" came the answer. "Straight turnaround, so if nothing goes wrong it should take four tides, putting us back here tomorrow night. "I'll get some gear and be with you shortly." We left Maldon under motor just on midnight and dropped anchor at Bradwell for a few hours sleep. When we awoke it was foggy, not dense but thick enough to be a nuisance, so I rigged the compass on its binnacle and worked out the courses and distances on a piece of scrap paper, using the new chart I had purchased recently. We saw some of the navigation marks I wanted, but by no means all of them. That did not bother me unduly, however hearing the ships moving in the Thames, as we crossed it did to some degree because we did not see one of them. I suppose that not seeing them was a blessing in disguise because had we done so it probably would have meant that we were close enough to court disaster. The mist lifted as we passed Garrison Point and the sun was shining by the time we let go at Queenborough. I landed our passengers and their chattels on the concrete ramp and we made our goodbyes.

I was just about to row back to the smack when a voice said: "What a' you doin' here," I looked round to see a fisherman I knew vaguely from over on the Leigh side of London river. We had at one time both used the same cold store and transport firm at Hadleigh. "I might ask you the same," I replied. "We're over here for the Trawler race, soot and flour fight, deck hoses, that sort of thing, we come every year," he said. "When's it start," I asked. "About half an hour." We then passed the time of day and discussed this and that for a while until he said that he had better go otherwise he would be late. I rowed back aboard, started the motor, hove up the anchor and we headed back downstream. The tide was not quite full so our timing was good for our trip back 'Down Swin'. Then I noticed several trawlers easing their way towards us. Oh no, I thought, I do not want to be the target for that lot. I opened up the motor flat out and was glad to see that our possible adversaries did not fancy a long chase.

It was now a hot, sunny day with absolutely no wind, as we motored back across the estuary. The sun, we thought, was strong enough to create an onshore breeze but it was late although the spiders who know better than we were spinning gossammer in the rigging, predicting the easterly to come. We were well into the Swin before a south-easterly finally allowed us to put up the gear and alleviate ourselves of the noise from below. Once it started it came more and more, eventually blowing the top end of a four bordering a five. Being a fair wind our speed over the ebb, once we were through the Spitway, was so good that we had to drop anchor just below the Big Spit at Millbeach to wait for water to Maldon. Like all summer onshore breezes it died with the sun and left it like a mill pond as we tidied the warps alongside the Hythe. As we were doing so, somebody said: "Thought you two were playing ferrymen to Queenborough?" "Been and come back," I replied. The next evening in The Queen's Head the remarks were: "Emmett, last of the sailing ferrymen, all aboard the Skylark for Sheerness," and "I've got two cows and a pig got to go to the Isle of Sheppey, can you take 'em as deck cargo."

As a postscript, a card arrived for me at The Queen's Head. It was from those intrepid cyclists which said that they were wintering in Portugal.

INTO BARGES

During that next winter Ray and I lived on board the sailing barge *Vigilant* whilst she was laid up alongside the Hythe at Maldon. The smack was derigged and laid on her bath wall mooring. With all the good will in the world, the idea of getting ahead with the 'jobs on the list' during the winter never happens. In the main it's outdoors, involves paintwork of some sort or is delicate finger work and the weather is just never suitable. The days are short and either damp or bitterly cold. To fill the time I attended an astro-navigation class which gave me problems to solve and books to read. At the same time the final draft of Blackwater Men was being typed by Gerry Courtney, with me dictating besides her as she typed for what seemed years, she asked me to expand on subjects, as we came to them, so that they would be explained better to the lay reader. The original hand-written manuscript grew by at least 50% owing to Gerry and the end result is due wholly to her tenacity and hard work. As the Spring arrived the barge work came along similarly to the

The Fishermen laid-up, all gear ashore.

(This page) Sailing Barge Vigilant.

(Opposite page) Gayle Heards mainsail accompanied by Valiants suit.

Valiant

previous year. Except this time I was asked to make skylight covers and a new main sliding hatch. It was as I was finishing the hatch that the owners and their friends turned up to take the *Vigilant* to Snape at the top of the River Alde. I told them that I was not quite finished but they said that they could not wait because the barge was due to be used for a wedding at the Maltings that Saturday. The owner, Martin, then said that if we did not mind going with them we could finish the jobs whilst underweigh.

Relieving a fouled rope at the masthead.

An hour later we were slipping past the promenade bound down the Wallet. Martin and his friends were busy rearranging some of the tackles and lower ropes around the mast case and left me to steer. As the barge would hold her course and the hatch was just in front of me I was able to finish that at the same time. By early evening we let go the anchor in the Ore just below Orford, having found six feet of water over or in-between, I should say, the shoals at Shingle Street. The passage up the winding river to Snape the next day was certainly interesting especially from the deck of a barge which appeared to be almost as long as the distances in the bends of the gutway.

Also during that winter I applied my brain to thinking about new sails, which were necessary if I was to ever get the smack to sail acceptably. My opportunity came when John and Roy, two good seasoned

Reminder, early to Maldon, half-brailed.

sailmakers helped set up a new firm called Valiant Sails. I approached them about what I needed and we measured for them. Then came some 'sitting down in the office type' talking, which resulted in their name being carried in both topsails as an advertisement. For my part it meant a handsome discount which made the idea come within my reach. So now *Ostrea Rose* had not only a new mainsail but a working staysail, No.1 and No.2 jibs, a tow foresail, a jibhead topsail and a large jackyard and clubstick topsail. Leaving the homemade spitfire jib as the only old sail.

Spring was the time when people started to return from their winter migrations. Some like Adrian Mulville from as far as the Caribbean, to where he delivers yachts. Others like Kevin Murphy had only London to travel from, whereas his girlfriend flew in from Montreal, Canada. The waterfront again took on a workmanlike appearance and the atmosphere cheered from those dark desolate days of winter. I used to be a winter person, whilst winkle gathering and herring drifting were to be done or even during the oyster company days but now I am going to admit it, adamantly, I am a sunshine sailorman by preference.

Although barge work had picked up for Kevin, he still came sailing on the smack and took a keen interest in developing her rig, sailplan and performance. Between us we cured her heavy helm and desire to stand in irons when trying to tack. The point at which we started was that of a vessel built as a motor fishing smack, ballasted from one end to the other and rigged with a mast meant to carry a derrick. The rudder was a barn door with a 'whale' size aperture in it for the enormous three-bladed propeller, and the sails, apart from the main, were nearly as old as myself and out of a variety of differing size vessels. The lists of jobs initially were long, at the end of every trial trip, gradually shortening, then the new sails arrived and the lists again lengthened. However, her performance and the feel of her movements improved inordinately. The day that was to be the memorable milestone was on a trip when we sailed into Brightlingsea Creek past the hard, rounded on to the other tack and sailed out again with the smack balanced to the point where, on the outgoing leg the tiller could be left unattended. It was the topsail that finally balanced her, without it she tended still to have a little weight on the tiller but nowhere near like it had been.

Returning one evening under our new rig we were gaining quickly on the *Reminder*, Bob Wells her skipper was in no hurry so he was half-brailed and just jogging up with the early flood towards Maldon. As we drew close, the mate, Roly, who was lounging on the forehatch beckoned and like a fool I sheared towards the barge. Suddenly through the air came a water bomb, then another, we'd been ambushed. "Get the mainsheet in, put the bo'line on, we're going round." We slipped out of range. "Got any bags," came the request. "Down below by the fireplace and while you're at it find a bucket we can hoist aloft, we'll fire down from the crosstrees." Meanwhile, we had positioned the smack for another sortie, this time at speed. As we drew closer the missiles flew back and forth, one as I remember it, finding its target right on a chaps chest, bursting all over him. I had one clip my head but luckily it did not spill its contents. We broke off to reload and reposition but on our next run we decided that having caught sight of them preparing the deck hose, we were severely outgunned and would make a tactical withdrawal. In the debriefing that followed between Kevin, Ray, myself, Bob and Steve it became apparent to us that those men who sailed wooden walls were actually worn out by the time they had caught each other, let alone then having to fight. As we got closer to the winding upper reaches Bob sang out for a tow as his engine was playing up so we put the smack on the port quarter of the barge and let Bob do the steering. Kate the cook had her daughter on board, and they were larking about saying

Pigeons past and present.

was it time for the rape and pillage. This was at the same time as Bob said that they had a good chocolate cake on board. We all elected for the cake instead; to which Kate said: "What a boring lot of pirates you'd make."

As we were making fast at Taylor's Sailmaker yard, where I was mooring that year, we saw a gull in obvious distress. Ray went off in the dinghy to fetch it and we found a can of pilchards below with which to feed it. When he returned with the bird I asked "What do you know about sick seagulls?" "That's as much as you know, I was in the RSPCA," replied Ray, "I'll clean it up and let it go." With that he took it to the houseboat *Black Pig* where he lived. What seemed like many days later I asked Ray what happened to the gull. "It won't go away, it thinks I'm a cheap meal, I keep throwing it up in the air but it just flies back again." A homing seagull, I thought. Talking of homing, we sometimes got landed upon by racing pigeons that were too tired to make it across open water. We had one crash literally on to the deck. It did not look well at all, just lay there pulsating for a good twenty minutes. Then it came to, drank some water we had put down and then strutted around the capping of the rail like a naval officer on the quarter deck of a First Rater. Finally, it sat on the mainsheet block lifting one foot every time the block neared the water, as the smack wallowed in the swell. In my father's album dating from 1947 there's a picture of a pigeon sitting on the compass, with a chap standing at the wheel behind it. The writing on the back of the photo says 'pigeon on compass with John Denulaine', then in small letters it says: 'JD went to Antarctic with Shackleton'. It amazes me how the pigeon seemed to have got star billing.

The other flying visitor is probably the one that makes me wonder the most. There you can be right out of sight of land and along comes a bee, they never stop, and never come on board. This creature is in theory incapable of flying according to aviation experts, it's just that nobody has told the bee, it seems.

STRING PARTIES, REGATTAS AND THE GREAT SWIMMING MOUSE

The man on the wireless had for some while used phrases like 'taking the heat out of the economy' or 'necessary trend' and had, I think, managed to persuade people that stagnation was the way forward. Well that's how it appeared in the charter world and on the lips of our charterers who were in business. It seemed as if we were heading for a 1930s-style depression and we did not wish to be depressed, so we decided to cut the cloth to suit the finance and enjoy the sun and wind. These I believe have, as yet, not been priced as a commodity.

The situation was to muster Kevin and several others for Shotley week. As I have mentioned previously I was moored at Arthur Taylor's yard, where I had neighbours such as Arrianne and David with a beautiful Edwardian yacht called *Freya* and Jack with his motor cruiser *circa* 1935. These liveaboards, like myself, created a nice community spirit. Other neighbours who visited regularly were Ed and Rosemary with the long, very sleek yacht, *Twiga*. On the morning we were to leave the weather was, to say the least, volatile. It had been raining heavily and persistently throughout the night with a nasty sou'wester on dark. When we awoke the wind had gone north west and although it was still precipitating, as the man from the Met calls it, there were signs of some sort of clearance. We made up our minds that we would go and so set the gear whilst alongside.

The, more or less, fair wind allowed us to sail off the berth. "See you in a week," I shouted. Jack waved and David returned a statement which I could not hear. We got very wet in the two miles to Mill Beach where the sun came out and killed the wind completely. "I don't fancy motoring all the way," I said. "Don't think we're going to have to, look back there," says Kevin. I turned and looked towards the north west, it was a line squall in the making. "Get that big jib off her, quick. I'll see about some reefs in the main." We were not finished but we were reasonably comfortable when it came.

Line squall in the making.

The wind hit so swiftly that it shook the gear violently before the smack was able to gather any weigh to absorb it. Also back came the rain and it too had violence about it. So much so that visibility reduced to fifty yards, which was not helpful as by this time we were reaching hull speed. I was confident of position and course for about five to six minutes before we may have found the mud but was not so confident of the whereabouts of the other vessels which I had seen before it shut down. Just as we were about to heave-to it passed and finally left us wallowing in sunshine, off the 'Doctor', considering the engine again. We surveyed the situation and concluded that another squall was not far away. We rigged the compass but found when the system hit us that it was of diminished ferocity and actually quite useful until it, like the last, left us wallowing. The whole trip remained like this with each squall being of lesser intensity than the last until it left us, once we were in the marina, with a wonderfully hot, sunny afternoon. We timed the trip, door to door as it were and made five hours ten minutes Maldon Quay to Shotley Gate, which is the best I have achieved with *Ostrea Rose*. At nearly six and a half knots, this for a boat of only a thirty-one foot waterline is a good average on passage, the norm being nearer four knots.

As we were cleaning Maldon's mud from the topsides with the

fresh-water hose, a voice hailed: "Can we lay alongside," I looked up to see *Freya* heading our way. "Jack's in the lock and Ed's hoping to come later in the week." We helped set the mooring lines and fenders for which we were rewarded with coffee and biscuits or should I say Dutch Straffels which Arrianne purchased on one of her visits home. The way in which I take my coffee always made David refer to it as 'a little black un'. "Well isn't this pleasant," says he, "Just like home at Taylor's." Having sat for a while in conversation suddenly Kevin says: "Beer time, Emit." "That's a little early for that, isn't it?" I enquired to which I received: "The man on the radio said we was all going to be on permanent holiday, so let's holiday make." There was no logical negative answer to that and so we went along the pontoons past the smacks and yachts, steamboats and sailing trawlers until we reached the marquee, inside of which was the bar. The marquee was close to the lock and from there we were able to see a barge coming through. "*Northdown*," says Kevin and we turned to the bar. It was decided to be extremely sensible and only have just the one. As the last dregs were tipped out of the glass a female voice said: "Hi guys, I'm glad you're here, do you want a drink." It was sister Sam, who by this time was about the only one with a job, she was third hand on the *Northdown*. "We promised to save ourselves for tonight," I said. "Oh, please stay, I've only just got here and I've had a rotten week and ....." "We'll have one Sam, you know me, I've got the worst no in the business," says Kevin, "and he's just weak willed". "Session on," states Sam, which started one of those evenings you always remember.

I make a great deal of mention in our travels of pubs and hostelries which may make it sound as if we are a bunch of alcoholics, so I am going to be very boring now and quote a few of our rules. We run a completely dry ship, except the odd glass of wine with dinner for the guests. Our 'runs ashore' never precede the necessity to sail the next morning or happen at anytime when the vessel is not completely safe at a mooring where personnel can get back and forth with ease. While I do enjoy a drink, I will under no circumstance tolerate or endorse drinking either at sea or in times prior to proceeding to sea. I have been known to turn down a charter on the grounds that alcohol was insisted upon being part of the day afloat. On one occasion I sailed at midnight with a new mate that I had been lucky enough to find at that late hour. The previous mate had been drinking and I would not sail with him. The sea is a place that is invigorating and inviting, it can also be a hostile environment sometimes at very short notice,

John Mellor, Kevin, Vicky and myself enjoying a string party.

where you need all your wits and strength to deal with it. Excuse me, I'll just climb down from my pulpit and return to Shotley.

The new sail wardrobe created an almost uncontrollable urge to be constantly sailing. Trying this and that, swapping gear round and discussing geometry and rigging with just about the whole world and its mother. Kevin nicknamed me 'short piece of string' owing to the fact I was always saying that that was what we needed for some job or another. When a rig first develops in a trial and error way, the tied up with string to see how it works syndrome is inevitable. This allows a list to be made and then the proper work to be carried out knowing definitely that that is where you need it.

One of our string days was to be a race starting at Pin Mill. Right we thought, to try this properly we need to be getting the gear set a little before the start, adjusting all this string until it flies correctly and be able to then judge her performance against other boats which we have previously raced against. So up the Orwell we go, spending the entire distance pushing and pulling, tying and slacking until finally we were totally satisfied and ready to take on all comers in the race. "What time's the start?" says Kevin. "Three o'clock," I replied. "Nice one, Emit, do you realise it's only a quarter to twelve," he complained. "We can't take that lot down now, we'll never get it back up again." "Well you're a man of many parts, though not necessarily all connected, you think of something," he retorted. I decided we would sail up to the Orwell Bridge and back again, and then again, oh, and again. Mainly to pass the time but we did time our fetches and plan our tactics. They say the best way to be late for anything is to be ready too early and this occasion was to prove that theorem Q.E.D. After being three and a quarter hours early we crossed the start line twelve minutes late.

Every evening in the marina the tools came out and repeated cries for blocks, lanyards, shackles or other assorted bric-à-brac went out to whoever would listen. Towards the end of the week the string had been replaced and the gear was becoming efficient, if still lacking certain large items. The absence of a proper booming-out pole, or setting boom as they should be called, was to prove fatal to another piece of equipment, the boathook. Long boathooks have unfortunately always suffered in the hands of traditional yachtsmen with delusions of grandeur. The poor old boathook of 10-12 feet is in the main, $1^1/_2$ inches diameter and is generally on board a vessel lacking a proper 15 foot 3-4 inch spar. Seeing promotion in the ranks the boathook steps straight in. Ours got promotion at Blood Point, after we gybed for the run up the River Stour to Ewarton Ness. We were going well and I was more conscious of our position with regard

The Orwell Bridge, again.

to other boats than of our gear. When Kevin says: "We'd best take that boom down." "Why?" I asked again without looking properly. Suddenly it flew into six pieces and buried itself unceremoniously at sea. "That's why," replies Kevin. Luckily I had another boathook similar back at Maldon and was also able to find a good setting boom to prevent further misuse.

Misuse was to occur again but on this occasion to something far more expensive and time- consuming to replace. It was to be the turn of the new topmast at the hand of Clive's Balloon Spinnaker. Who's Clive? you ask, well that's a story all on its own so we will have to return to the spinnaker later. At the end of the previous season's festival I found myself, as did a lot of owners, without crew to return home with. Crew that year came as and when, and in-between barge work. That job being erratic to the point where Kevin was called at 0530hrs from his bunk on *Ostrea Rose* offered work and was bound away half an hour later.

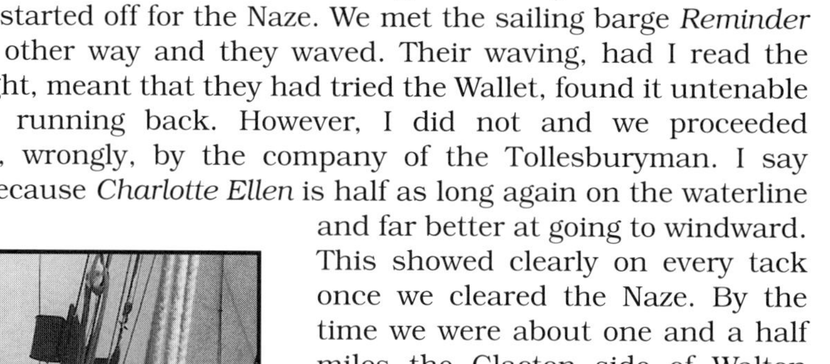

The weekend in question that should have seen the south bound fleet home, was as bad a summer gale as I have seen. Many did not venture out and on reflection I should have been one of them. However, we locked out behind the big Tollesbury smack *Charlotte Ellen* and started off for the Naze. We met the sailing barge *Reminder* going the other way and they waved. Their waving, had I read the signals right, meant that they had tried the Wallet, found it untenable and were running back. However, I did not and we proceeded comforted, wrongly, by the company of the Tollesburyman. I say wrongly because *Charlotte Ellen* is half as long again on the waterline and far better at going to windward. This showed clearly on every tack once we cleared the Naze. By the time we were about one and a half miles the Clacton side of Walton pier *Charlotte* was out of sight. It was here I noticed that one of the starboard shrouds had parted company from its lanyard. I decided to run back. That as it turned out seemed to be easier said than done but it had to be done because we had run out of tide, and therefore could no longer make it even if we had wanted to.

Lizzie Annie under our setting boom, showing us her heels. This fast little oysterman, when owned by Dick Wright, once swung flood at Fambridge, fetching Maldon on the same tide.

After four attempts, unsuccessfully, to wend her round in the steep short seas she finally went. This was as we were closer to Gunfleet Sand than I wanted to admit even to myself. However, we were now going in the right direction but the weight of the wind seemed to have increased even more. I watched as a tiny split in the foot of the staysail ran quickly along leaving a gaping hole before I had chance to do anything about it. Back in the tranquil surroundings of the marina I repaired the damage and tidied up. Whilst I was doing so the reports of events other than ours were filtering along the pontoons. A smack sunk at Pin Mill, a yacht was lost on the Gunfleet with the crew airlifted off, strained hulls leaking and so on.

All this made me bring to mind a saying that I had heard: "It's far better to be in here wishing you were out there, than to be out there wishing you were in here." However, the adage horses for courses always proves true because much later I saw Lenox Leavett and asked him if they got all the way home with the Charlotte. He looked at me blankly and asked why I thought they should not. That's the difference between a river smack and a true estuary ranger. So there I am crewless and asking around but as I have said everybody was in the same position. I got talking to Maggie Lamb, who I had met the previous year at the festival, and she said that a chap called Clive would be in the bar that evening who might help out. I entered a very much quieter bar that evening and was pointed in the direction of a sizeable chap sitting at the bar with a woman who had an alsatian at her feet. I introduced myself and put forward my problem. His answer was quick and precise: "I'll do it if Christine and Cat can come and you can get us back by road." The road transport I knew was not a problem because David Plummer on *Freya* had always said that anytime I needed the van I only had to ask. So I said: "That's no problem but why do you want to bring your cat." "She doesn't like to be left behind," he expanded pointing towards the alsatian. I must have looked like I doubted his word or something for he said: "Sit up, Cat, give me your paw," and the dog responded. Thinking of the Barry scenario and the countless others that had been on the boat, I thought I must be like a magnet for these type of people. Still they do say that like attracts like 'birds of a feather' and all that.

The next day we locked out into a three reef north westerly but with the promise of better things to come in the sky. As we sailed out of the harbour the wind was noticeably dropping, as it continued to do until Clacton pier where there was none and the motor completed

the journey. It seemed that as the wind decreased, the jokes and the one liners increased from Clive which sparked me off. This led to Christine eventually to plead: "No more for goodness sake," and I swear at one stage I thought I saw Cat, the alsatian, go to put her paws over her ears.

I borrowed the van on arrival at Maldon and delivered my crew back to their hometown. We made our goodbyes, saying that we were bound to meet again and I left.

To return to the year in question and the topmast incident. We sat in the bar, having a relaxing time, when the door opened and in walked a figure in shorts, a very loud shirt and a head-dress that looked like 'sheikh your money'. "Hello Dad, I knew you were here, I saw your zimmer frame parked outside." It was Clive.

The next day we were to race from Pin Mill again. The race course was normally to a different place each day such as the Walton Backwaters, Mistley on the Stour or Ramsholt on the Deben and so on. The reason, as I remember it, for using Pin Mill twice was that the north easterly had been just that bit too much for the Deben Bar and the River Orwell provided a more sheltered sailing alternative. The second race from there was the programmed one and in fact found a mellow day. Clive came aboard in the lock with a kit bag that looked full enough to last a month. "What on earth have you got there?" came the question. "Warrior's spinnaker," he replied, "I thought we'd try it and give 'em a run for their money." For those who may not know, and that included me at the time, a Warrior is a very much bigger vessel than *Ostrea Rose* and has standing backstays and compression stays. A long boomed, gaff cutter's standing rigging is totally different and not geometrically designed to do the same job as the Warrior's. However, when boys get together it always turns into 'piece of string' time. It must be the English innovator in us coming out. The plan was to set the spinnaker from the topmast head and sheet it, well, we had not thought that far ahead by that time. We rounded up off Wolverstone and up it went with a wind so light it would hardly lift the flag at the masthead. She almost instantly picked up full speed. I mean it was exhilarating, "Yes, I mean No! get it down, look at that topmast." It was bent under compression and looked like an 'S'. The sail collapsed sideways as they are prone to do and almost caught hold of the starboard summer crosstree. Luckily

Clive in yet another disguise.

(Opposite page) 3 reefs to the Naze.

Comparisons of what should be set and what should not.

When Maldon still had regular shipping.

it missed because I hate to think what that would have done. Finally, it was inanimate on deck and a few seconds later was banished to the sail locker in favour of gear more suited to our rig. It did show one thing though and that was the tremendous power available in sails of that kind. No wonder the modern racing fraternity have gone in that direction leaving the long boomers in the comparative backwaters. I must admit that I feel more at home in the latter after all's said and done.

It was whilst jilling about waiting for the start that a phenomena, I had seen before at Maldon, occurred to the largest extent I have witnessed. When a sizeable vessel, especially one whose draft is nearly equal to the depth of water, is moving in a confirmed inland channel it sucks the water away from the edge quite considerably. The result is a returning surge after its passing. At Maldon when the ships still brought timber from the Baltic to Sadd's Wharf I have seen the Bath Wall beach run dry and then resubmerge, with the barges at the quay ranging back and forth straining against their springs. We were making a fetch up the north shore just downstream of the Orwell road bridge, keeping outside of the channel buoys. We did not have a vast depth of water but we were sufficiently afloat to move. Ipswich at that time had two extremely large ships the *Nordsky* and *Nordsee* working there. It was to avoid being a nuisance to one of those that put us where we were. As the ship passed we grounded and watched the edge dry travel towards us. We waited a short while and true to pattern the water returned, the smack lifted and we sailed on.

The Ellen on a glass sea.

The next time Clive was to sail with us was during an Old Gaffers East Coast Race in the Blackwater. The most memorable part of that race, which was run on a day with very little wind, was the jokes and general banter. A young chap named Guy, who was on board, actually pleaded for us all to stop because his stomach hurt from laughing. At one stage a particular crack seemed to touch the nerve that creates hysterics. It was after we calmed and collected ourselves that we noticed we were by then pointing in exactly the wrong direction; Serious racing! Kevin when at work was sailing the barge *Reminder* but on this day along with his girlfriend Vicky was sailing on *Ostrea Rose*. Whilst he was playing tactician, and I use the term advisedly, he was looking through the binoculars. "Have you spotted *Reminder*?" Vicky enquired. "No, I painted her grey," came the answer, and so the day continued.

Up until very recently Kevin Murphy was the only person I have ever let sail *Ostrea Rose* without myself being on board.

Even at the time of writing there is only one other but that is for later. It was Osea Race and I had been saying all summer to Andy and Jayne that I would have a sail with them on *Ellen*. We were getting *Ostrea* underweigh when Jim Lawrence passed under our stern with the *Ellen* and Jayne shouted: "Well, are you going to come and sail on a good boat, then?" I thought about it and turned to Kevin: "She's yours to race, put me aboard there."

As *Ellen*'s gear was set up and they already seemed to have a complete foredeck complement under the command of Andy, I went aft to talk to Jim and to direct my charm towards Jayne in the hope of obtaining a cup of coffee. It seemed almost coincidentally that the moment I stepped on board the wind failed. "A piece of ballast on a line," said Jim, "We'll hang it over the stern to hold her pointing downstream and heave it the second the guns gone." It worked a treat and for the first time I was on a boat out in front. Now this causes problems, it means that you have to know where you are going for one thing because there's nobody to follow.

The office of tactician fell on me and for once I had to take it seriously which meant looking only where we were to go, not worrying about looking behind because we had already been there. It was about level with the Nass when Jim said: "Have you seen your ship lately, Master." To which I said: "No," without turning round. "Well, I suggest you have a look," he continued. I peered through the fleet

The powerful Tollesburyman "Charlotte Ellen".

until there was my underrigged little oyster dredger looking like a Beken of Cowes image. Kevin had the lot set. The wind by this time had increased to a good breeze and I'm thinking, "Please not my topmast." We in the *Ellen* unfortunately, after such a good start, had to retire but it meant we could return to a relaxing anchorage at the Island, where we sat on deck watching the participants crossing the line. When *Ostrea* came in although she had no place, she was creaming along with all gear well trimmed looking like a winner.

Having been on Christopher Kerison's races in the Colne and heard the feedback about how popular that race was, I decided to organise a race for the upper reaches to Maldon to complement the already established Colchester race. With the help of a young chap called Jason we made plaques for all entrants and I fashioned a slightly larger one, with a native oyster on it. It was a very informal affair. I hand wrote some instructions and photocopied them, then distributed them amongst the owners by post. The day dawned, and the fleet bigger than I had even hoped for, turned out at the Nass. The bang came out of the Maldon Little Ship Club cannon, which we had borrowed, and off they went. The race was to be in three stages: The first leg finishing at a line by Southey Spit was to be a boat for boat sailing race. The second leg was the dredging match where the first smack to catch a native oyster off the Maldon Several Fishery and transfer it by means of her pulling boat to *Ostrea Rose* would be the winner. The last leg was the first smack home across a line at the quay. All went well until the *Charlotte Ellen*, who was out in front, grounded in the middle of the channel in Basin Reach. "Unfair," they shouted. "Bang," we shouted back, "You've won and you're now the line." The rest of the fleet brought the flood tide with them and we moored on the mud outside The Queen's Head. Here we held the prize giving and the rest as they say is history.

At a time somewhere in the middle of that summer I had a three-day cruise with some people from a village eight miles inland from Maldon. If variety is the spice of life they certainly achieved that goal in that timescale. The first day was a stiff three reef breeze tramping up the Wallet, the second was a whole sail light air dribbling up the Blackwater and the third was a glassy calm.

(Opposite page) The start of the smack race for the Maldon Town Cup, as Televised by Anglia in their 'Sail Away' series. Left to right, Laura, Sallie, Sunbeam, Saxonia and Peace.

As there was absolutely no chance of any sort of wind, whatsoever, we decided to motor from our anchorage off the island up to Maldon. Here we resurrected the old clinker-built pulling boat, bringing her out of retirement. Most of the contents were put in the skip and we collected enough sweeps with which to row her. This done we set off

CK 328

back for the island where we would scrape off the barnacles and weed, with her turned upside down on the beach. I think a lawn mower would have been of some value, whilst the barnacles seemed like they were ganging up on us. Eventually we won the battle and victorious we set off for Goldhanger Creek where we intended doing some rill inspection. We took the smack up 'Earl' and let go the anchor. I was back in my mind, to the days of winkle gathering and how what we were doing now, used to be so commonplace. We all got into the skiff and everybody took a sweep except me. I stood in the stern sheets and pushed with a pole.

We travelled up the main creek which bends to the left and meets Bawley's Creek draining from the saltings on the island. Here we took a smaller gutway that splits the mudflat right along its centre, with the main Earl to its left and Stumble drain to its right. Nearer to the Island's half tide causeway, all three join to become one again. At intervals along the gut that we were in, were minor joining gutways in both directions. It was one of these we were to take through into Stumble. As we did so we looked at the weed and winkles, whilst flounders left little explosions of mud powder as they struck off the edge into deeper water. In Stumble are some 'piles' protruding out of the mud, as there are in both Earl to the south and Wages Creek to the north. They are remains of ancient fish traps or 'kettles' as they were once called. "Fish," I started, "and another." The mullet were playing along the edge of the mud which led down to Earl Spit. By now we were level with Joyce's Creek and close to the ground used by the new oyster firm for growing Pacific Oysters known as Gigas. They lay them, not like we used to the natives, under the low water mark, but above it in 'French Parks'. This gives the appearance of a well tended allotment. We pulled steadily on because I wished to clear Earl Spit and be in its main channel before the flood made a hard pull of it. The smack was just starting to drag her chain up the creek as we boarded for afternoon tea.

I dropped down into the cabin and started passing the necessaries out of the companionway, so that the engine hatch could become the buffet table. It was as I was lighting the gas under the kettle that I heard one of the ladies on deck say: "Oh look, there's a little mouse," in a voice you might have expected to be reserved for babies in perambulators. I shot out of the hatch like a human cannon ball. "Where?" I demanded. "You're not going to kill it," the woman said indignantly. "No, of course not, but it can't roam free on here, they gnaw these type of sails cruel," I explained. "It ran in there," she pointed to the waterway under the bridgedeck where the winch used to be sited. "Got him then, block both ends and I'll get the lard net that I used to use for winkles." I put the net over one end and some water was flushed down from the other. We all saw the mouse enter the net and yet it was not in it, nor was it still in the waterway. "OK, I give up, how did it do that?" I remarked. "There it is by the stern," somebody said. I looked and saw it but instantly it was gone again. The great disappearing mouse, I thought, that's all I need. "Now where is it?" I asked and everybody looked blank until a voice said, "There, in the water." True enough it was swimming, making a tiny bow wave, towards the edge-dry.

As we watched I remarked that I did not know that mice could swim. Suddenly a great thrashing happened in the water and the mouse leapt clear of it. "Mullet," I exclaimed. "That will eat the poor little thing," came from one of the women. "I doubt it, they more likely disturbed and frightened each other," I added. "You'll have to go and rescue it," the woman insisted, so now she's rowing and I'm like Captain Ahab only I'm armed with a lard net instead of a harpoon. We neared and I scooped the animal out of the brine conscious to be quick as it had already once been small enough to escape capture by passing through the mesh. I need not have worried on this occasion for the tiny creature had exhausted itself and lay quite still. Several minutes later it revived so I put it upon the mud where it ran off at great speed towards the island. It definitely knew where it had to go and kept that conviction until we finally lost sight of it.

The old fishing tales, like the one that got away, where the hands held apart defy size or logic, never seem to die out. It was in The Queen's Head one Sunday evening that several of us sat in the window seat of the 'member's' bar dissecting the weekend's business. Two strangers came in and bought a drink. Their conversation was of a trip they had just come back from. Apparently they had been on an angling boat out of Bradwell and by all accounts had caught some fish, but like all good anglers could not resist the time honoured gesticulation. Waterfront pubs, certainly on the east coast, create the ability in people to converse, even with people they may not know. It's an old-fashioned social intercourse which seems to be dying out further inland.

Now David Plummer, a gentleman in the very best sense of the word, leaned across and introduced himself in his soft spoken Norfolk dialect explaining that he was a boatbuilder from that county and that he once had occasion to go trawling on a boat out of Lowestoft.

He had been reminded of it by their conversation and hoped that they did not mind him butting in. They said of course not and asked him about his trip. Well, he said, it was all going fine until the net came fast on a wreck which took a long while to free. Once they had managed to retrieve the net though, they saw that it was a very old wreck because there was a Roman lantern in it and the wonder was that it had a candle in it. Moreover, it was still alight. He paused with everyone thinking what on earth is he talking about then he says: "Now, if you take a foot off your fish, I'll blow my candle out." The ensuing laughter came also from our new friends and they spent the rest of the evening with us.

The first time I met David, his girlfriend Arrianne had asked if I would sit and chat with him during the day. Apparently he had just been operated on and must not move unduly for several days. This was causing him untold boredom and as I knew exactly what that complaint was like I went to *Freya* with some sympathy. "Come aboard, you'll have to make the tea, I mustn't move," says David. I made the tea and we chatted about this and that until I saw a timed opportunity to enter the latest joke I had heard. Poor David was in trouble, he made noises and hand movements which I obviously took to mean stop saying the quip. He was near to bursting with laughter and it was hurting. Luckily we calmed down and he returned to a more comfortable situation. I then asked what the operation had been and he said: "A hernia, I got it laughing at some silly ..... telling me a joke."

In the summer preceding the time of writing I managed to catch a mullet of about 4-5lb in weight. We had been at Wolverstone and seen a reasonable size shoal feeding around the pontoons. The weed and other growths seem to be in abundance there. A young lady who was with me became very taken with their presence and wanted to catch one. However, the run of the shoal had finished before I had chance to sort out the implement of capture from below decks. So our chance was lost but we only had to wait until the next day to be offered another. We had sailed back towards the Blackwater and had decided to break the journey at Brightlingsea. We moored against a high-sided steel trawler opposite the hard. As we were tidying the warps she said: "Michael, look, there's a fish in-between the boats." I gazed quietly over the side making sure not to disturb it with my moving shadow. It was feeding more or less head to tide and was in the dark shadow held by the trawler. Holding the stick handle I gradually lowered the lard net into that shadow and in front of the fish. I kicked the bulwarks sharply which startled the quarry and it shot forward into the net. I lifted it quickly tipping the catch on the deck. The inevitable inspections, questions and so on came from the guests on board. As I picked it up by its head and tail someone said: "What are you going to do with it?" "This," I answered, as I dropped it back to the place where it would obviously feel happier. We watched as it gathered its senses for a second and then disappeared into the deep.

That had been the first fish I had caught since decommissioning, apart from the desperate dinner with Melvin, and I actually felt sorry for it. I am sure, when I think of the many hundreds of stones of fish we used to catch and market over the years, that it is the ardent hunter who becomes eventually the most passive conservationist. In conversation with David Stoker from West Mersea recently he asked if I did any shooting, to which I replied no, none at all. He then went on to say that he did not either and that he preferred to see the wildfowl flying about the place. We both come from families whose livelihood contained large dependency upon professional wildfowling.

....

NOW MISTY THE PLACES, SOFT FOCUS THE FACES BUT NONE OF THEM GONE WHILST YOUR MEMORY LIVES.

GOOD TIMES AND HARD TIMES, HUNGER AND PLENTY, SWEET LOVE AND DEEP SORROW, FULL LIFE HAVING LIVED.

THE WHISPERING TIDE.

Les Brown, River Blackwater 1996.

CHANCE MEETINGS

During the patient endurance that winters demanded, I spent most evenings in the 'members' bar of The Queen's Head. The conversation and antics were much more preferable to sitting night after night, in a little box watching an even smaller little box that sits in the corner. As interesting as some of the productions may have been, which emanated from that source, it did not make for meeting people or broadening horizons in social contact. The barmaid, Christine, referred to herself as a 'little owd granny' but had a sense of humour that I could really appreciate. Entering the pub from a windy and very wet street in my wet-weather gear on one occasion attracted the comment: "Not the sort of night to be cast adrift in an open neck shirt," to which I answered: "No, and I'm not looking forward to the journey home neither". One evening as I sat talking to her a fellow came in and asked for Michael Emmett. I looked at him and said: "Does he owe you money?" to which he replied, "No," so I claimed, "Well that's me then."

(Opposite page) Maldon Waterfront.

Edith as we found her at Melton Boatyard.

Apparently he had been talking to some people in the Jolly Sailor about his meanderings looking for a boat to buy. In his story he mentioned that although he and his girlfriend had started by looking for a yacht, they had in fact come across a rebuilt smack which had really taken their fancy. Someone in that gathering then told him, by all accounts, that he should talk to me; for some reason? We exchanged pleasantries, during which I learnt that he was an Englishman, naturalised Dutch. His girlfriend, Carey, was Dutch and they lived in Amsterdam. He quickly ran through their general travels in search of a boat which had led them to Mel Skett's yard at Melton near Woodbridge. Here they found what appeared to be a rebuilt smack-yacht called *Edith*. She looked good in appearance as far as she went, but was a long way from being finished, he said. We discussed smacks and boats in general for a long while, then he says: "Would you have a look at her and give us your opinion." I said I would and asked him when he would like to go. "Unfortunately, I return to Amsterdam by tomorrow morning's ferry, so could you let us know by post and by phone what you find?" he replied. We agreed upon the course of action to be employed and I received telephone numbers and names of people I would have to contact. He visited for coffee the next morning, made his farewells and drove off to Harwich to catch the boat.

I made the necessary arrangements by 'phone and travelled to Melton by train. That journey always makes me think of what all the 'crab and winkle' lines must have been like pre war when yachtsmen from London were able to visit their yachts at Tollesbury, Brightlingsea or Maldon, by catching the train. The line runs from Ipswich to Lowestoft, bye Woodbridge it passes within feet of the mud in the dock. It then follows the river to the little station at Melton having almost dissected the boatyards on its progress. Here I alighted to be met by the yachtbroker who drove me the very short distance to the yard. Painted pale blue, with varnished cabin sides, that had portholes which lacked the fittings, the pole-headed little smack lay in the mud alongside a very much larger smack, *Rhodda*. I boarded and instantly appreciated what Richard had told me. It was good and solid but nowhere near finished. I poked around for a while until I was satisfied I had seen all that I wanted to on the first visit. On returning home I telephoned Richard and told him my thoughts and suggested he had her lifted out so that we could view her bottom. Whilst this was being done I also suggested that he asked David Plummer to inspect the engine. This was carried out the following week and a deal was struck on the basis that Mel Sketts was employed to carry out some preparatory work to the engineering. This was necessary to enable her to be brought to Maldon where more permanent work could be undertaken, prior to being taken to the Netherlands.

It was during the same period, and in The Queen's Head, that I was to make a chance remark to a young lady that was to change my life. "You'll have to come sailing sometime," was what I said, and as I remember little more was broached on the matter. Richard telephoned me at The Queen's Head and announced that he would be coming over within a couple of days. He asked me if I would assist him in jury rigging *Edith* and sailing her to Maldon. I said I would sort out some of *Ostrea Rose*'s gear and be ready to travel to Woodbridge as soon as he arrived. We spent two days treating *Edith* to the biggest 'piece of string' party I have ever been to, whilst the holes without ports had plywood disks bolted inside and out to make them seaworthy. Satisfied we had covered most eventualities we returned to *Ostrea* where we were to have about four hours sleep before returning to Melton for the 03.30hrs tide. I, by coincidence, met the young lady whose name is Deborah Cannom and said: "We're sailing tomorrow if you fancy a trip?" "What time?" she enquired. "Two o'clock at the quay, we're driving to Suffolk." I suppose if I'm honest I really did not expect her to turn up at that hour but at five minutes to two a shadowy figure shouldering a ditty bag walked along the wharf.

Deborah.

It was just breaking daylight as we finished loading this and that from the car and let go the warps. I went astern out of the berth, got clear and put on ahead propulsion, with the tiller hard over to turn her. However, she instantly wanted to return to the berth. I looked around for obstructed lines and could see none, so I put her once again astern to draw clear. On putting ahead the same pattern evolved. Then I considered her quarter propeller and looked to see that the engine was actually central. The story my father related about the ketch *Lady Hilda* started to ring bells. In her, every time the ahead propulsion was engaged she would pin the stern hard against the quay at Poole. It was due to the shaft being at an angle to the ship's centre line and exasperated by the hand of the propeller. I had inherited the same problem and so decided to let the smack drive sideways with the young ebb until we reached the bend in the gutway where we could use the propeller to drive and overcome its effects by steering against it.

This was my first trip down the Deben and I was quite surprised how tightly packed the moorings were. I was to utilise this knowledge at a later date when arriving at Woodbridge in the 48-foot smack, *Pemberth* under full rig, rounding up into the wind between the moorings in the bend under the trees, with just myself and the owner Graham Brewster to scramble the gear off her. We motored on in *Edith* through water that you could see your face in, down passed Ramsholt where the pub nestles in the trees and overlooks the river until we reached Felixstowe Ferry. Here river pilots still exist but we pressed on without, having taken local advice at Melton about the bar which seems to have a life of its own. The weather could not have been any the more perfect so unless we did something very silly our passage should prove effortless. In the event it was and we were soon making slow progress against the ebb towards the Naze and I passed the helm to Richard, who had been acquainting himself with the area by reading East Coast Rivers and studying a chart he had purchased. Debs by this time had made an armchair out of the space between the bitts and the stemhead. I asked Richard if he was happy with steering to which he said that if he needed me he would give me a shout, so I went forward and chatted to Debs until we reached Mill Beach only two miles below Maldon. We gained just a little breeze towards the latter stages and were able to set our rig up. This brought several remarks, not all necessarily polite but funny nonetheless. Finally, we berthed her alongside the *Ostrea Rose* so that Richard could live aboard her and work on *Edith*, for the duration of his stay. The day after he had to return to the Netherlands I put Edith on my Bath Wall mooring where she was to reside quietly until the next visit of her owner.

Jury Rig.

HISTORY AND HUMOUR

In the weeks that followed Deborah and I were to sail *Ostrea Rose* purely for our own enjoyment. Trade was thin but it did not matter for this is a way of life not just a way of making a living. They say that things always come to those who wait and that the Lord provides in manners other than money. People close to the land and water appreciate the wealth accumulated in stores that are not quantified by the current accepted means of exchange. Finance, for instance, does not create happiness and we were happy. Having said that, Deborah did on one occasion raise the age gap of nineteen years between us. I challenged her calculation because I was forty and she twenty-six, leaving only fourteen. "Yes, I know I'm twenty-six but you've got the mental behaviour of a seven year old," she claimed. "That's nice, again," I said in mitigation, whilst I began to realise that this very quiet person I'd met had caught the waterfront disease of inane humour.

Waterfront humour is in its timing and subject matter quite unique but seems to be timeless in its application. The form and direction so common at the time of writing is remembered also coming from the 'owd hands' and the generations in-between. One such character that springs to mind is Douglas Stoker who during conversations about the water added: "do you know that was so rough one night that we spent three hours on just one wave," and, "When I was young I went to sea with the Grandfather and do you know we were that poor that we were kept at sea for six months because we couldn't afford a mooring." Coming more up to date I looked at Kevin Murphy once and asked: "Is it legal to be as ugly as you?" to which he answered, "I'm a mirror." Talk about caught by the live-in glasshouse and throwing stones scenario.

Richard returned from the Netherlands to carry out more work on *Edith.* Carey came with him this time and treated us to some of her Dutch hospitality; fetching coffee, Straffals, tobacco and all manners of small gifts. We spent many breaktimes lounging on deck discussing the future developments which were to happen to *Edith* whilst also trying to piece together her 'provenance'.

Richard and Carey.

Carey showed me several documents they had managed to obtain. They proved that she had in fact been built as a fishing smack rather than a smack-yacht and traced her working life into the 1930s. From then on she disappeared off traceable record. I mentioned that I thought she was too high sided for a working vessel and that her topside shape would have made her a difficult boat to work. Then Carey showed me some photographs and ran through the details of her later history. Apparently the boat had spent twenty-five years in a farmer's barn being gradually restored as a project for a spare time hobby. During this period she had been raised by two planks and the tumblehome accentuated in her topsides. That answered my question about her hull but left a time gap of some thirty years during which nothing seemed to be known. We explored many avenues, all returning blank, until one opened up before us when we were not actually looking for it. I was exhibiting at the London Boat Show with the Essex Sailing School. The principal, a friend of mine, Mike Tyrell, had agreed to let me use part of the stand in return for my labour. Pictures of *Ostrea Rose* hung on the wall of the stand along with written information and all kinds of people chatted and discussed all manner of sailing aspects. An elderly gentleman approached the stand one day and said: "I used to own a smack something like that one but I doubt you will have heard of it because it was in very poor condition when I owned it in the fifties and I would imagine that it was broken up years ago." "What was she called?" I enquired to which he replied: "*Edith.*" He was so pleased when I told him that she had not met her demise but rather she was being restored, if altered, and that I was looking after her in Maldon. "Oh Maldon," he added, "My son has a Maldon boat now, she's called *William*, have you heard of that one." The *William* was built for Bill

Wright, the one they nicknamed 'Slosher'. His son, Jack, who inherited the same nickname worked her with his brother Arthur, whom they called 'Lucker'. Jack's son, Alan, worked both with my father and myself, on and off, for long periods. So it was equally pleasing for me to hear that the old *William* was still in existence.

Carey and Richard toiled tirelessly through the mountainous list of jobs, whilst they also scoured every source of second-hand traditional equipment which they needed to get *Edith* sailing. She was starting to take shape but they, like Kevin and I had previously, became resigned to the hard fact that the only way to obtain a proper sail wardrobe was to have it made. Valiant were once again called in, and a set of sails made from white material arrived not all that long after. I helped bend them on and agreed to have the first shake down trip with them. Like all new rigs it was the string syndrome, so after we reached the clearer water down river of Southey Spit, we came hove-to to gradually replace it. The smack stood on station, steming the tide for nearly the whole duration whilst we altered shackles, leads, screwed on thumb cleats and so on. We bore away twice to find that although we had reefs in she laid down rather more than that required and needed therefore a lot more ballast.

Her slight bilge was already almost full and this made Carey and Richard decide to have an external lead keel fitted. I'm not a lover of external keels as they require bolts that tend to rot away, as my father found when a twelve ton lead keel fell right off his vessel, luckily alongside Maldon quay. This at least did allow it to be picked up by a crane, from where it was transported to James and Stones yard at Brightlingsea and refitted. My other preference to well pegged internal ballast packed right up into the turn of the bilge is one of motion dampening when rolling. However, this was not my vessel and everybody has their patent preferences. "Different boats, different ideas," as the 'owd hands' used to put it. *Edith* received her new keel at Heybridge Basin prior to making the North Sea crossing to Amsterdam. She was to be moored underneath the window of Carey and Richard's abode in that city. This story seems to be one that might have had a timescale of say three to four months from purchase to crossing. However, the Maldon magnet that always draws people back, if indeed they ever go away, was to prove very powerful over our Dutch friends for it was to be over two and a half years between those two events and during this time they were to become known as regular waterfront inhabitants, they even joined the sailing club. It was sad to finally see them depart but we still keep in touch.

Helga passing the Royal Yacht.

The morning sun enjoyed by the author and John Linton the navigator after a long night.

It was in the summer of the *Edith*'s first arrival that I attended the enormous festival of maritime affairs at Brest and Douarnenez. It was also one of my rare excursions into those new fangled boats without a spar at the head of the sail. The triangular piece of cloth was rigged on the most beautiful 1930s yacht owned by a friend from the south coast, John Lesh. John is the man that you will always take notice of where shanties are being sung close to a boat because he's the one with the stuffed parrot sewn on the side of his hat. It seems like the south coast has been riddled with this headless sail disease but I'm sure that given therapy like that which I administered to John, will make the rest, like him, see the error of their ways and return to the gaff fold. "Alright, nipper," he would say in his true Hampshire accent, "You'll just have to pretend that that gaff is there, until I can do something about it." Now, nipper, there's a thing, on the east coast I'm regarded as Dad, perhaps these triangular sailors have got endearing qualities after all.

This was my second visit to Brittany, I had been there four years earlier when the festival was held purely in Douarnenez. On that occasion I was in a Baltic trader named *Helga*, who was rigged as a square topsail, gaff schooner. It was whilst in her somewhere down towards Weymouth that I first saw a 'J' class underweigh. It was the *Velsheda* and she passed us almost as if we were standing still. These trips and festivals require a book of their own and we do not have the space here, unfortunately, to dwell longer.

Question: If the wind was West and West steered we.
The wind was from behind.
How could that be? **(ANSWER OVERLEAF)**

RACING TO THE SUNSET

The next season was to be one full of racing, some serious with poor results, some light hearted with better results and some treated with total flippancy that drew first prizes. It started early in the season with Deborah entering *Ostrea Rose* for a race against modern yachts belonging to Maldon Little Ship Club. We mustered for a start line at Bradwell that proved impossible for us because it was short and crowded. Our slow manoeuvrings, hindered by the wind dying completely meant that the ebb tide swept us passed outside the limits. Cats paws and faint whispers held us looking at a very patient Bernie Barratt whilst he awaited our painful attempt at struggling back to the line. At least twice I said: "There's no point, they're out of sight, look!, we'll never catch them," and was nearly banished below by the determined crew. Deborah led the constructive

Dressing the bottom on Osea Beach.

ANSWER TO RIDDLE: The skipper's name was West.
He came from Colchester

A drifting match (L.R Marigold, Ostrea Rose, Fly, Good Intent, Sunbeam).

revolt, followed by Melanie and a recruit, engaged from the retired ranks of Her Majesty's Royal Navy. Ian Cox, or 'Buffer' as he is known to everybody including his friends, had helped us with the fitting out. Give him a polish rag or a paint brush and I believe he could make a showcase job of a destroyer on his own in less than a week. Smacks were small fry to him and he was invaluable to us, in far more ways than would have been contemplated, as will become clear later. Finally we were able to point in the right direction.

Within a very few minutes we were afforded a nice breeze just slightly east of south, which meant we were on our most effective point of sailing. A quartering breeze, sheets eased slightly and all set from jackyard to tow foresail and watersail. It seemed like we had been given the wind first, for we were creaming along towards that fleet of fifteen vessels which had been out of sight, watching them appear one by one. As we bowled along down the Wallet we overtook several and could see the leaders. They, by this time, had gained the wind and maintained their distance on us.

Away to the south east was a funny heaviness in the lower sky but we still had good sunshine in our vicinity. "Rain," somebody said just as the temperature dropped rapidly and the heaviness made alarming progress in our direction. "Get the compass up, that's fog." No sooner had I said it than we heard the other vessels sound their foghorns.

"Best get ours," I asked. It arrived on deck with the box compass but despite being tried by different buglers the little Dutch pattern foghorn was unwilling to toot. "That's because you haven't bothered to clean it," gibed one of the girls. Buffer by this time had transformed from a painter into a human foghorn and was honking out, one long and two short, better than a Canada goose.

We turned to find the beach which I intended to follow using the long pole to sound with until we reached Walton pier. The first apparition was the lifeboats boarding skiff, we were not sure if we had missed the lifeboat itself or whether she was out. We were not allowed long to linger on that subject before the pier loomed high above our deck and required us to turn hard to starboard to avoid ending up as an appendage to it. As we rounded the end we passed the time of day and had a short conversation with some anglers. This was cut short by coming upon a yacht from the East Anglian Sailing School called *Strata IV* which was imitating our course only going in the opposite direction. The ladies on board had seen some hilarity mileage to be had out of cleaning the foghorn which by this time you could see your face in. What I am going to say now is honest; Melanie put it to her lips, blew and it worked. "There you are, all it needed was cleaning." Realising that I was totally outclassed I retired to the more mundane task of navigating. We were still blessed with a good breeze although the visibility was negligible. I estimated her speed at around four knots and set a course to clear the Naze ledge. We sounded regularly with the pole, feeling rocks now and again until eventually, and more or less coinciding with my timing, we dropped into deeper water. Here we changed course setting towards the groyne at Blackman's Head. I erred on the side of Dovercourt rather than the channel in case we missed and got mixed up with the shipping. We sailed on for what I deemed longer than my estimated timing, until we could hear dogs barking and people talking. Then out of the fog came a wooden lighthouse, had we slipped back down a time tunnel, no it was the disused one at Dovercourt.

My time discrepancy was due to not allowing for the young flood which had just set against us and eventually had driven us sideways. No matter, far better that than being without a solid mark and wondering if you are about to be run down. Also estimating a sailing vessels speed accurately is difficult for winds vary in force and it relies to some degree upon judgement by eye. A very simple method of obtaining a calculated speed is the 'Dutchman's Log' and is most useful in the event that external aids, either do not exist or are out of action. A piece of wood is thrown overboard at the bow and the time taken. When it reaches the stern (LWL) the time is recorded again. With this information a small equation is entered; multiplying the length (L) by 6 and the time (T) by 10. The resultant time is then divided into the length which produces the speed of the ship in knots. Thus:-

$$\frac{6xL}{10xT} = \text{Ship's speed in knots}$$

This may seem crude but it works very well in practice.

We picked our way around the groyne and along passed Harwich, taking a chance on the short nip across the mouth of the Stour where lash lighters and lightships laid to give us good position identification. Finally, we locked in only to look round and see the cranes of Felixstowe, the fog had gone as quickly as it had come. The race had been organised by Tommy Mills for MLSC and in that capacity he visited us bringing a glass tankard, announcing that we had come second for that leg of the race. The second leg was to start off the Shelf at Harwich the next morning with a finish line at Bateman's Tower in the Colne. Odin was certainly smiling on us, a nor'easterly at the top end of four. She just about carried her jib headed topsail comfortably, for a quartering breeze all the way, running now and again. This time we had visual contact with our competition and were extremely satisfied with another second place which brought us a glass tankard to raise our winnings to two.

We were to use Shotley quite a deal that season, basically because it suited our purposes better at that time than Maldon. Deborah had always impressed me with her ability to learn, and her natural aptitude towards sailoring, but it was that lock gate that was to prove her real worth. We were approaching the dredged channel, marked by the two posts under main and two headsails. I said that I would take the jib out of her and run the bowsprit in, if she would steer. I was just tidying the last rope when a post went past. Knowing that the channel was only yards long I let the mains down to about two feet above the boom and peaks to suit so they were still set. Pulling the staysail aweather with the bowline I let nearly half of that down as well. I glanced at the lock gates, which were open and the operation lights were green. "When are you going to start the engine?" came from aft. "No, no, you started it, sail her in!" I turned and picked a warp off the hatch to use as a spring. As we crossed the line of the

Valiant SAILS

Opposite:
An old trawlerman's trick, a topsail over a 2 reefed mainsail.

Top:
The tension of racing.

Bottom:
Graham Brewster.

gate, I dropped the peak on to the deck inside the bulwark and let go the staysail, which flaked itself over the bitts. I then managed to catch a turn on a cleat, on the fender skirt of the lock, surging the smack to a standstill. A professional piece of seamanship on her part being able to enter a cross tide lock such as that. Sadly it was witnessed by only me and the lockmaster, for apart from us the place was deserted.

As I have mentioned before the best way to be late is to be ready early. The reciprocal of that you might think is impossible, well, so did I. However, the two rivers race which starts by obtaining your instructions from the Butt and Oyster was the exception that defied the logical rule. We were of course late for the briefing, I mean what's new, I was thirty-two days overdue when I was born, ask my mother, according to her I've been late ever since. So as we arrived ashore, everybody else was departing to prepare for the start. Graham Brewster, owner of *Pemberth* had sailed with me whilst Deborah had gone in the bawley *Bona*. "I fancy a pint of shandy," he said, "We're not going to get anywhere because we're late already." I tended to agree with him and the rest of the crew looked as laid back about the situation as hot sultry windless days can make you. We resigned to have a pint, watch the rest of the fleet rush around and then get underweigh for a dribble back to Shotley.

Running down to Levington.

By and by we rowed aboard and set the gear. Letting go of the mooring we sheared out into the tide and gazed down river toward the fleet of about forty boats strung out on what looked like a mirror. The tide drove us nicely, whilst now and again a tiny cats paw would waft us along. It was soon apparent that we were overhauling even boats that we should not be able to and it was due to being lucky to catch airs that they just were not. The other element that was becoming plain as a pikestaff was that this heat was going to create an onshore breeze which would come with the flood tide. It was now touch and go whether we reached the turn mark at Blood

Pembeth crossing the Hawrich Breakwater finish line with Avola being committee boat.

Point with the dying embers of both the northerly airs and the ebb. The tension was unbearable. Graham said later that he could tell I was getting serious when I had the skiff pulled on deck and had everything prepared for the reach up the Stour. We were laying the wrong side of the buoy for the tide and we could see the wind coming up through the harbour. We tacked for a short one to lay the buoy and clear two other boats. Tacking again, up went the tow foresail and we were pulling along on the edge of the new wind.

We saw the leaders up ahead, the greyhounds, *Ellen*, *Sallie*, *Bona* and so on, all with their gear yet hanging limp driving up with the tide. We were closing fast and were within shouting distance at the Ewarton turning mark. Then the windward leg let us down as it always does against these longer sleeker smacks that drag no propeller. Our competitive adrenaline, however, prevailed and we carried the jackyard the rest of the way although the north east wind had now reached nearly a five. As we steamed over the line with two of us on the tiller everybody on board felt that we at least had a place in the ratings. It was to work even better than that, our differential of handicap was just enough to overcome the four boats we could not catch and therefore it brought us the cup. *Ostrea Rose*'s first ever. We had a small celebration that evening!!

Classic Boat week is the time to sail other people's boats as much as your own. For instance Graham, had only just turned Pemberth out after a twelve year restoration and was finding all those teething troubles that Kevin and I had experienced on *Ostrea Rose*. It seemed sense to have a sail on her one day and give him a list of alterations he needed to attend to. This list was long with my suggestions being added to by all the other owners. I have sailed *Pemberth* since and she is much handier but like all boats she could still benefit from a little something here and there. It never stops in reality. I had known *Pemberth* back in the sixties when an unfortunate collision between her and a south coast smack named *Fanny of Cowes* caused considerable damage. It was at the mêlée of the start of the East Coast OGA race in the Blackwater. I remembered it well but had seen neither vessels since, which made me wonder, when from the deck of *Pemberth* I saw the *Fanny* sailing down along the opposite shore in the Orwell.

Another vessel we were to sail that week was the Lowestoft smack *Excelsior*, probably better described as a sailing trawler. A mate of mine, Robin Cassel, was skipper at that time and had invited us out for the day. Unfortunately the fickle winds of high summer do not suit a North Sea trawler of seventy-seven feet L.O.D. with a winter rig in

EXCELSIOR
Picture by
Colloryan Ltd.

Everything set.

it. So we had a lovely day drifting about and then left her on the mooring outside the lock entrance, going ashore in her liberty boat. I was later to go as mate in her for a fortnight's trip, which amongst other places took us to Amsterdam. In the marina that year was a vessel I had wanted to buy but was unable to, just prior to having *Ostrea Rose* built. Fate is a funny thing, had I bought this other boat, the *Quiz*, my tubby little green Maldon bawley would not exist. However, Paul Webster was as keen for us to sail with him as we were to try his smack. We took the tow foresail and watersail from *Ostrea* and set off for the Deben rally which was to culminate in a race from the offing buoy at Woodbridge Haven back to Harwich breakwater. As we cleared the marina entrance channel we set the gear up and I said: "What's that funny noise" "Funny noise, what funny noise?" came the answer. "Oh, I thought that sounded like the kettle boiling." I was told off by Deborah for being so cheeky on someone else's boat but when I need coffee, needs must and all that.

It was as the drinks were being made that Paul asked me to go below to look at something he did not like the look of. I dropped down below and was equally not impressed with what I saw. The mast had a scarf in it, in the worst possible place, where it passed through the deck. It appeared that the glue had given up the ghost and luck was supporting our mainsail and two headsails. As she nodded in the slight swell the scarf opened and closed. "Can you get me some line and a piece of rod or something," I requested. "Do you want the sails down?" Paul asked. "No, I think with this step at the bottom of the scarf, which incidentally ought not to be there, a Spanish windlass will probably hold it because the top has a mast band." We applied the 'Heath Robinson' which seemed to work fine so we pressed on for the Deben. We knew, as usual, that we were late so we decided not to enter the river but wait for the others to re-emerge for the start at the Haven. The time spent waiting was used to picnic whilst hove-to looking at the moderate breeze from the north east. It was then that the day's deliberate mistake became apparent - we had forgotten the setting boom and it was a running race from beginning to end. The only boathook on board was less than five feet long, so even delusions of grandeur were out of the question. We took it in turn to try to make the tow foresail fly, using the short boathook to extend our short arms. It was no substitute for a fifteen foot spar but we were able to get the sail to draw, if a little inefficiently. For all that we were able to hold third place over the finishing line.

A race which *Ostrea Rose* won boat for boat was started in the Walton Backwaters with a time elapse start to give slower boats a chance. We were allowed ten minutes on some and twenty on others, whilst about ten boats started with us and another slower class was sent off ten minutes earlier. The course was out to Pye End, off to the Stonebank, down to a mark laid on the Cork ledge. Then back to Harwich breakwater leaving the shipping channel port hand buoys to starboard. It struck me that the start was only just before high water and that the full ebb of the Wallet would be running across the Medusa enhancing the ebb running out of the vast area concealed in the backwaters. The course from Pye End to the Stonebanks would therefore mean having this direction on the beam and with the wind slightly south of west it would be very doubtful in one fetch. Also any windward work would then be against the

Jon Wainwright's, Nobby Deva.

tide. We rounded Pye End and stood back more or less towards where we had come from. The rest of the boats with us stood off for the Stonebank. If my calculations were right we had a severe weather gauge.

Then I noticed we had company, one other vessel had decided to join us, it was Jon Wainwright in the little nobby *Deva*. Jon is a local man, well Mistley, so I'm sure he was quite familiar with this rouse. We stood into Pennyhole Bay until we nearly had to take up inter-tidal residence. After we had tacked the buoy looked easy to lay on that fetch and Jon was comfortably astern of us. We were only some hundred yards from rounding the buoy when the wind eased to such a degree that the tide which we had just entered sloshed us sideways and put us the wrong side of it. Up until that last few yards we had been sheltered from the full effects by the Naze ledge. We tacked and tried to regain the last fifty yards or so, whilst we watched *Deva* seemingly laying her course nicely. Then it caught her which made Jon tack. We struggled on against the tide watching every inch. It seemed ages, especially seeing the handy little *Deva* only a few yards to leeward of us. Finally we thought we had clearance and tacked, she made it but it was close. It was all effort to boom out as much canvass

Blackwater Women (Deborah and Melanie).

as we could crack on her. Once we could do no more I took time out to look at *Deva*. She was only a hundred yards behind and we had a lot of course still to cover. It was almost like doing the tango with her for the rest of the race, she would gain and then lose. The nearest she got was about twenty yards and the furthest about a hundred and fifty yards behind until at the line we saved around eighty. The helmsman, or woman I should say, was Deborah for the entire duration and she made a consistent job during a long race. That ebb tide caught the rest of the fleet badly and many did not even complete the course.

Lily May fetching down 'Pont' to Bradwell on the morning of the Oyster Race.

Deborah was to find her first command in the Lynn-built shrimper *Lily May* during the Maldon Oyster Dredging Race. She not only had the task of sailing the vessel but also hand dredging under sail to catch native oysters. The race itself which I had organised previously in a very impromptu fashion had by this time gained support from both our local authorities. They had paid for shields and trophies to be specially struck for the event. It was also to be televised, the film being made by a chap called Malory Maltby and his son. I had met Malory on my last trip to Brest, he was on an old RNLI vessel now named Redundant Hero. The day may not have produced a place for *Lily May* but it had produced the best kind of ambition in a latent character.

"I want to be a skipper," was the demand. It came something like a week after the event and had taken that amount of time to be digested and considered before that statement was made. Deborah at that time was foredeck crew of the highest quality but it was a far cry from her desired goal. "If you're serious I'll help you, but once we start there's no stopping," I told her. The ensuing months were constant study, question and answer. A great strain on any relationship and I must admit it had its moments. She doggedly persevered, as I just will not accept jobs left unfinished. Eighteen months after that initial statement, in appalling April weather, she and two lads from the barge world took *Ostrea Rose* away for three days. They picked an examiner up at West Mersea and returned with Deborah holding a Yachtmaster Offshore fully commercially endorsed certificate. As I have mentioned earlier one person other than Kevin, has been

Winning Skippers at the prize giving for 1993 Maldon Town Regatta.

(L.R) Oyster Trophy: Fisherman Ben Woodcraft sailing John Rigby's Sunbeam.

Maldon Town Cup (1956): Sailmaker - Gayle Heard sailing Laura.

Maldon Town Shield: Bargeman Richard Titchener sailing Sallie.

Maldon Rock Trophy: Rupert Marks sailing Hyacinth.

The 1956 cup was won in that year by the authors great uncle Ernie who at eighty four years of age was sailing the family's smack Polly.

allowed to take my smack away without me and that's Deborah. In fact for a season when I was busy elsewhere she ran the boat completely at her discretion.

Where did *Lily May* come from you might ask. Well, we sat on deck one evening eating dinner when a character I had not seen for years turned up. Looking up at him, standing on the quay I exclaimed: "Lord, look who's here, do you know I heard you was dead!! As you're not you had better come aboard." The gentleman in question was Richard Emans who whilst supposedly at school, actually preferred to be covered in herring scales on the *Mollie*. We had not seen each other pretty well since that time, which led to some fairly rapid coverage of events pertaining to the time elapsed. He had done very well for a truant, it seemed, by owning an agricultural engineering business. Unlike me, he had seen the lack of financial gain in working on the water and had migrated right away from it. Preferring the more lucrative rewards of the land. There are snags in all choices, however beneficial, especially in a character who has the salt-water bug. You can turn away, move away, live long periods away but that bug laying dormant under the skin will always return you. "I want to buy a smack," he says. "You're mad," I replied. "I've got enough to be able to afford to have a toy and I've seen one, will you have a look at it for me?" She was moored at Brightlingsea and had been brought down to the lower berths for us, so that we could take her for a sail. At that time she was a half deck, long welled boat with no auxiliary engine.

(Overleaf): David and Goliath OR should I say Deborah and the Dutchman.

Valiant
5

Compared with *Ostrea Rose* she handled like a dream, if a little flighty. She was in need of more ballast, in fact we found out later that some had been removed during her rebuild and had not been replaced. I thought she was an ideal little boat in good condition, which is what I told Richard. Only a few days later he informed me that he had made a deal and asked me if I would fetch her to Maldon for him. In the event the delivery ended at West Mersea, for he changed his mind due to finding out about the end-of-season racing.

Richard Emans aboard Lily May

There was a nice breeze on the day we collected her. In *Ostrea*'s terms, a whole sail breeze with a bit of life to be felt in the hull. I was to get a reminder after years of working tubby, stiff vessels that narrow gutted boats just will not carry the gear in the same way. The wind piped up a little and I was at first amazed at how she heeled heavily as I hung on to the tiller. Like I was used to with mine I hung on but unlike mine she laid down even more and washed four oars off the side deck. Man overboard drill times four and we did not lose a single one. We reefed and sailed into the quarters as far as the wind would allow us. It was straight out of the reach by the packing shed. Having picked up a buoy I said: "We've a small problem, how do we get ashore, we've no dinghy and the launch seldom comes right out here." "No problem, I'll 'phone the club," says Dick. "We haven't got the number," I remarked. "Where have you been hiding, haven't you heard of directory enquiries?" he added, pressing the buttons on his mobile. During the few minutes that we had to wait for the club launch, I mulled over the changes. The 'owd hands' I knew as a boy were lucky to have a serviceable primus stove and now smack owners had telephones. The launch arrived driven as usual by Fred, or that's what I have called him, without contradiction for something like thirty years. It was to be a charterer the following year that remarked: "Why do you call him Fred?" "Because that's his name, everyone I know calls him Fred," I replied. "That's strange, his name's Jeffrey," said the charterer. Perhaps his dad's name was Fred. I mean the son sometimes inherits the fathers nickname or they are referred to as old so and so, and young so and so, then there are times when the second name is used in preference as Clem Last did, his initials were J.C.L.

We were to sail *Lily May* several more times until Richard said:

Sailing Barges at Maldon.

Cabby has Hay's in her mainsail. The light grey one underweigh is Reminder, whilst the dark one is Portlight. Between them and dwarfed is the little Cygnet.

"Will you race her in the oyster race?" to which I replied, "No, I can't, but Deborah can."

Hanging around the waterfront is a world apart from the accepted social behaviour of the vast majority of people today. For instance, we get more casual visitors in the course of a day than most people in houses get in a month. It costs me a fortune in tea and coffee. I mean, how many people would pop into your bedroom, while you are in bed and discuss business or just pass the time of day. It seems open and inviting enough on the boat for people, who would not dream of doing that at a house, not even to give it a second thought as to it not being acceptable. It's this social contact that appeals to me, especially in this day and age where people seem as if they are becoming very solitary unapproachable units in little boxes with triple locks and spyholes. I have always run an 'open house' and will strive to maintain that. The other anomaly is the total ignorance of time, accepting that of the tide. For example, I was walking on Maldon quay one Sunday morning when Gerard Swift said to me: "What are you doing this week?" "Not a wonderful lot," I replied. "Well you are now, we're going to Antwerp." So out of the blue and pretty well immediately we were bound down the Orwell with the sailing barge *Cabby*, which Gerard is the skipper of. I suggest that a lot of people would be of a mind not to want such erratic alterations to the pattern of their lifestyle. However, it is this sense of variety that makes it for me.

Early in the season containing all this racing lark, we were asked to attend, and be an exhibit at, a boat show. It was to be held at Burnham Yacht Harbour on the River Crouch. Our involvement started with press day which required sailing up and down the Crouch in company with other exhibitors. Mike Tyrell was there with his Sadler 32 which he runs in his Essex Sailing School, Roy Hart had his ex-America's Cup challenger and so on. The weather apart from the wind direction, which was southerly, was abysmal. It rained continually and blew hard enough, not that you would have thought so if you had seen the footage because it did not look bad at all. In fact, it made you wonder why everyone was wearing waterproofs. We tacked about and reached up and down sometimes in close enough quarters that we could step from one to another. In fact Mike started playing with our topping lift at the end of the boom which was over his deck. Needless to say being a soft eye fitting over a shoulder, it came off in his hand. The two helmsmen then had to keep together until we had refitted it. It made for a new connotation on running repairs.

In the marina we were allocated a berth and asked to supply trips as a 'Get afloat for the first time' promotion. This we did making six one-hour trips each day throughout the four days of the show, using the engine on only five occasions. Each day at 1300hrs we were to be the exhibition victim for the 999 service demonstration. We were given a smoke machine which when set off made the boat look as if it was on fire. Flares were let off and a liferaft launched, into which we climbed. The lifeboat and paramedics then arrived to take away a casualty in a Robinson stretcher.

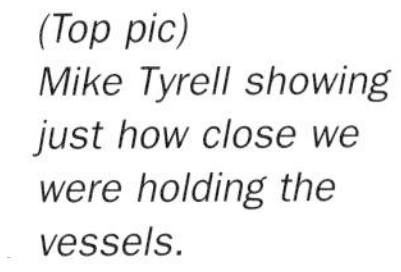

(Top pic)
Mike Tyrell showing just how close we were holding the vessels.

(Bottom pic)
Smoke, Flares and Ham acting

The Ham actors led by Buffer (kneeling). The Thistle in the background was the only spritty sailing barge built north of the border

Buffer was leading hand in this caper because he had been through all this in the Navy, but oh, the ham acting, it was appalling, no it was embarrassing but enjoyable and we did get ovations. It was hard work but a thoroughly good week as all weeks are on the water.

On the last evening of the show, which after its bad weather start turned out to be the best you could have wished for, we sat on deck lounging and talking. A bugle note struck from somewhere across the marina, instantly Buffer was at attention and saluting. The rest of us looked across to see what was going on. A cadet training yacht run by the RNR was calling sundown and lowering the ensign. It amazed me to think the training which must have led Buffer to recognise and respond at such an instant. I will leave you with the image of Petty Officer Ian Cox, RN, retired, at attention on my taffrail saluting the ensign as it lowers.

AN ESSEX IDYLL by A R Emmett

(written at anchor in the Blackwater in 1947)

The yacht at anchor stemmed the flowing tide,
Which rippled gentle music all its own.
The tinted sunset, dying in the west
To leave the twilight hour to me alone.

Then I could sit and contemplate at ease
And smoke my pipe, remembering what was past.
The flight we made to claw from off the shore,
The mounting seas, the line squall moving fast.

How scores of little finches, skimming waves
In hard, courageous struggle toward the land.
And many, in their need to catch their breath
Alighted on my rails, close at hand.

The wailing cry of curlew rent the air,
With many other sounds I could not name,
Unearthly and forlorn perhaps they were
I felt I knew and loved them just the same.

A spritsail barge drifts slowly passed my gaze,
Her tanned sails limp before the dying breeze.
Her skipper waves to me a cheery hand
And drifts passed unhurriedly, at ease.

The startling crash of some duck-hunter's gun
A thousand sea birds' voice a loud protest,
These things, to city folk of no account,
To me great memories, and still the best.

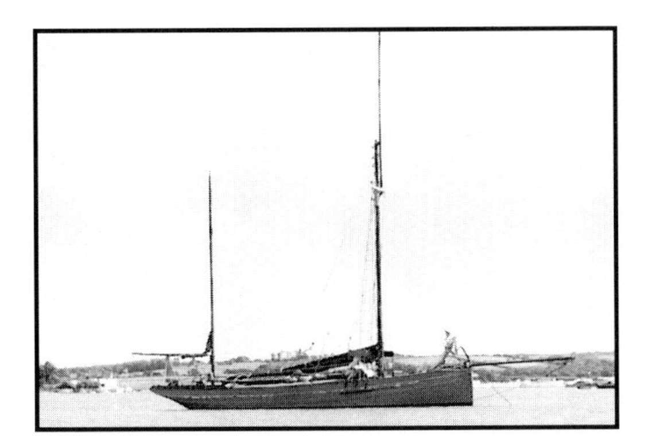

BOOKS FOR FURTHER READING

BLACKWATER MEN by Arthur and Michael Emmett
"This book is a fascinating, inspiring and sometimes humbling story of tight knit community of watermen"
Chay Blyth CBE BEM @ £14.95 plus £3.05 P&P U.K.

TRADITIONAL SAIL: A panorama of heritage.
Compilation of well-known authors by Michael Emmett
"to preserve and promote our maritime heritage.... a contributor to our future prosperity"
John Whittingdale OBE MP @ £3.00 plus 99p P&P U.K.

English Estuaries Series by Robert Simper
(Creekside Publishing 1995)

Vol 1 Deben River
Vol 2 River Orwell and Stour
Vol 3 River Alde, Ore and Blyth
@ £12.50 each plus £3.05 P&P U.K.

Vol 4 Essex Rivers and Creeks
Vol 5 Norfolk Rivers and Harbours
@ £14.95 each plus £3.05 P&P U.K.

Send cheques made payable to: Gaff Rig Publications
125 High Road, Layer De La Haye,
Colchester, Essex CO2 0EA. Telephone: 01206 738187

Prices as at time of writing and therefore may be subject to revision.